With Love & [illegible]
To ~~[illegible]~~ .

Christmas '91.

~~From [illegible].~~

D0991530

# PREHISTORIC SCOTLAND

# PREHISTORIC SCOTLAND

## ANN MacSWEEN
## MICK SHARP

B.T. Batsford Ltd London

*For John and Rhoda*

Text © Ann MacSween, 1989
Photographs © Mick Sharp, 1989

First published 1989
All rights reserved. No part of this publication may be
reproduced, in any form or by any means, without
permission from the Publishers.

ISBN 0 7134 6173 X

Typeset by Servis Filmsetting Ltd, Manchester
and printed in Great Britain by
Courier International, Tiptree, Essex


for the Publishers B.T. Batsford Ltd
4 Fitzhardinge Street, London W1H 0AH

# Contents

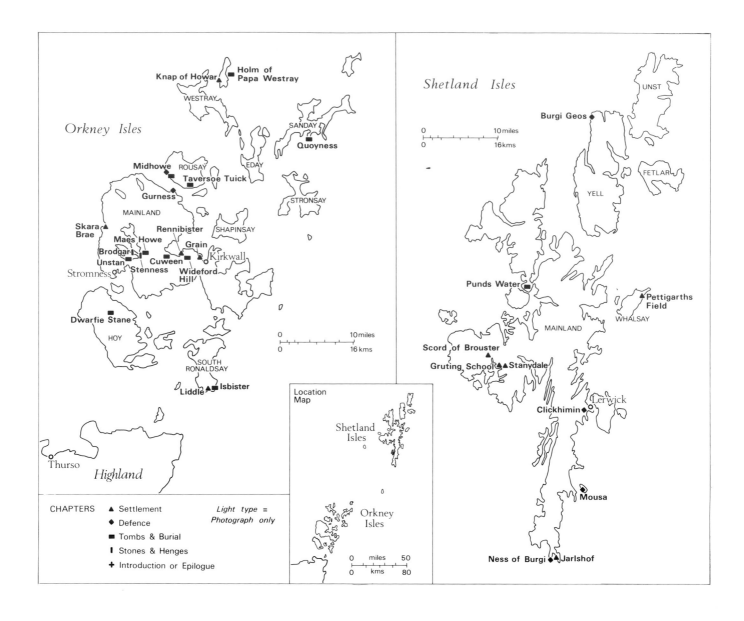

**Orkney Isles**

Knap of Howar  Holm of
Papa Westray
WESTRAY
SANDAY
Quoyness

Midhowe
ROUSAY  EDAY
Taversoe Tuick

Gurness
STRONSAY

MAINLAND
SHAPINSAY

Skara
Brae  Rennibister
Maes Howe  Grain
Brodgar  Kirkwall
Unstan  Cuween
Stenness  Wideford
Hill
Stromness

Dwarfie Stane
HOY

SOUTH
RONALDSAY
Liddle  Isbister

Thurso
**Highland**

CHAPTERS  ▲ Settlement
◆ Defence
■ Tombs & Burial
❙ Stones & Henges
✚ Introduction or Epilogue

*Light type =
Photograph only*

Location
Map

Shetland
Isles

Orkney
Isles

0   miles   50
0   kms   80

**Shetland Isles**

UNST

Burgi Geos

0   10 miles
0   16 kms

FETLAR
YELL

Punds Water
Pettigarths
Field
WHALSAY

MAINLAND

Scord of Brouster
Gruting School  Stanydale

Lerwick
Clickhimin

Mousa

Ness of Burgi  Jarlshof

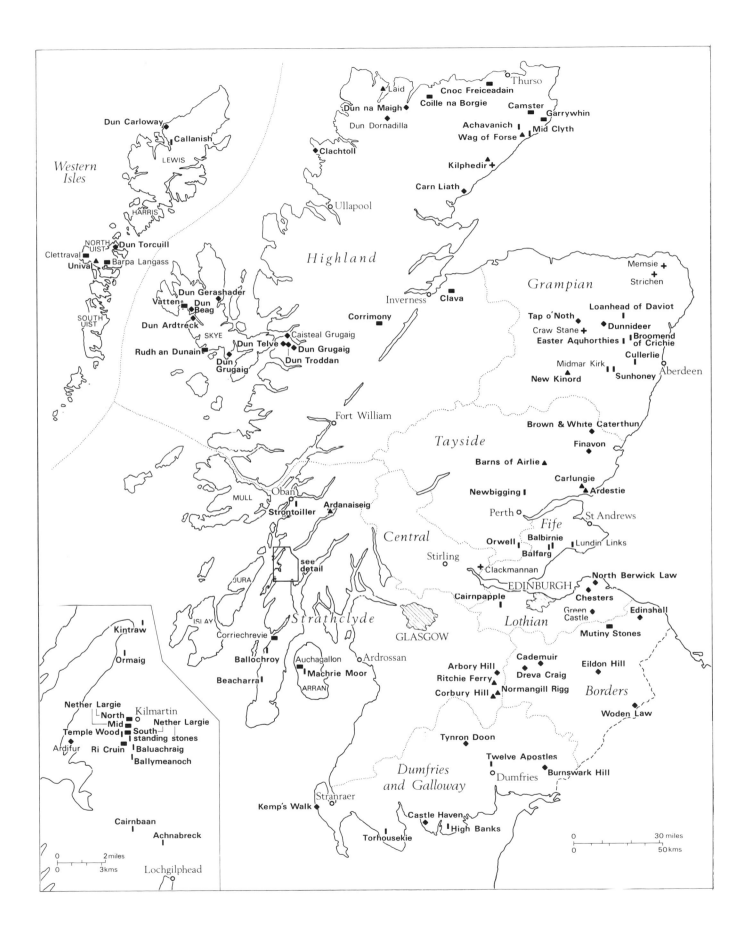

**Western Isles**

Dun Carloway ◆
● Callanish

LEWIS

HARRIS

NORTH ◆ Dun Torcuill
UIST
Clettraval ■ ▲
Unival ● ■ Barpa Langass

SOUTH
UIST

Laid ▲ ● Thurso
● Laid
Cnoc Freiceadain ■
Dun na Maigh ◆ Coille na Borgie ■
Camster ■ Garrywhin ◆
Dun Dornadilla ◆ Achavanich ▲
Mid Clyth ▲
Wag of Forse ■
Clachtoll ◆ Kilphedir ✚

Carn Liath ◆

Ullapool ○

**Highland**

Dun Gerashader ◆
Vatten ■ Dun
● Beag ■
Dun Ardtreck ■
SKYE
Caisteal Grugaig ◆
Rudh an Dunain ◆ Dun Telve ◆◆ Dun Grugaig ◆
Dun ◆ Dun Troddan ◆
Grugaig

Inverness ● Clava ■

Corrimony ■

**Grampian**

Memsie ✚
Strichen ✚

Tap o'Noth ■ Loanhead of Daviot ■
Craw Stane ✚ ◆ Dunnideer
Easter Aquhorthies ■ Broomend
of Crichie ■
Cullerlie ■
Midmar Kirk ●
New Kinord ● Sunhoney ■ ■
Aberdeen ○

**Tayside**

Brown & White Caterthun ◆
Finavon ◆
Barns of Airlie ▲

Carlungie ▲
Newbigging ▮ Ardestie ▲

Fort William ○

Oban ● Ardanaiseig ◆
Strontoiller ▮
MULL

Perth ○

**Central**

Stirling ○

**Fife**
St Andrews ○
Orwell ▮ Balbirnie ■
Balfarg ■ Lundin Links ▮
Clackmannan ✚

North Berwick Law ◆
EDINBURGH
Chesters ■
Cairnpapple ▮
**Lothian**
Green ◆ Edinshall ◆
Castle
Mutiny Stones ■

**Strathclyde**

JURA

see
detail

Corriechrevie ■

Ballochroy ■

Beacharra ▮

Auchagallon ●
● Machrie Moor
ARRAN

Ardrossan ○

GLASGOW

Cademuir ◆
Arbory Hill ◆ Dreva Craig ◆ Eildon Hill ◆
Ritchie Ferry ▮
Corbury Hill ▲ Normangill Rigg ▲
**Borders**
Woden Law ◆

Tynron Doon ◆

Twelve Apostles ○
Dumfries ○ Burnswark Hill ◆

**Dumfries
and Galloway**

Kemp's Walk ■ Stranraer ○

Castle Haven ■
Torhousekie ■ High Banks ▮

**Inset (lower left):**

Kintraw ▮

Ormaig ▮

Nether Largie
Kilmartin
North ○
Mid ▮ Nether Largie
Temple Wood ■ South ■
standing stones
Ardifur ▮ Ri Cruin ■ Baluachraig ▮
Ballymeanoch ▮

Cairnbaan ▮
Achnabreck ▮

Lochgilphead ○

0 ___ 2 miles
0 ___ 3 kms

0 ___ 30 miles
0 ___ 50 kms

# ILLUSTRATIONS

# FOREWORD

Scotland's prehistoric monuments have long been a source of interest to locals and visitors alike. Some have been extensively excavated and researched; others remain enigmatic.

In *Prehistoric Scotland* our aim has been to provide an introduction to Scotland's prehistoric sites, using specific examples to illustrate the various monument types. The sites which we have chosen to highlight by no means constitute an exhaustive list. The choice of some sites, like Skara Brae, Callanish, or the Glenelg brochs was obvious; others were chosen because of excavation evidence, associated historical detail, or photographic potential. Still others were chosen purely because they were personal favourites.

The book begins with an introduction to Scottish prehistory, a summary of the various periods and the current state of thinking. The dates throughout the text are calibrated radiocarbon dates. Many are approximate and will change with future research.

Following the introduction, the chapters are arranged thematically – settlement, defence, burial and ceremonial being the broad topics covered. The divisions are sometimes arbitrary – some 'defensive' sites such as hillforts were also settlements, some 'ceremonial' sites contain burials. Each of these chapters begins with a short introduction which is followed by a selection of sites. Within a chapter the sites follow in roughly chronological order where possible, and are grouped by site type. Although each entry can be read separately, most background detail for a type of site will be found in the first entry for that monument type.

The book ends with a short epilogue, a gazetteer and a glossary of archaeological terms.

Rather than put together a traditional guide book, we have tried to convey – through illustration and description – something of the mood of the various sites. Mick's photographs capture the atmosphere of many of the sites by portraying them in their landscape setting, as well as providing details of their architectural characteristics.

In describing the sites, the aim was to go further than the archaeology where possible. After their original use, many archaeological monuments have a second 'life', as objects of fascination to visitors, and the focus of local folklore and legend.

In addition to the text and photographs, each chapter has been supplied with an 'imaginative reconstruction' by Jean Williamson. Jean used excavation evidence combined with her own ideas of prehistoric life. Her drawings add the human factor which is difficult to portray by text or photographs.

Ann MacSween
Edinburgh 1989

# ACKNOWLEDGEMENTS

The authors wish to acknowledge the 'Historic Buildings and Monuments, SDD', particularly Jenney Hess, Senior Information Officer, for arranging access and photography of sites in their care on Orkney and Shetland. Thanks to the custodians at Jarlshof, Maes Howe, and especially the friendly and helpful crew at Skara Brae. Also thanks to the staff of the University of Edinburgh Library, the University of Bradford Library and the National Library of Scotland in Edinburgh where most of the research was carried out.

We also gratefully acknowledge the following people who aided the photography and fieldwork by their advice, practical help and hospitality:

Philip Abramson, David and Lois Anderson, Rosemary and Tony Baker, Donna and Phil Cunningham, John Harcus of Kirkwall Campsite, Christina and David Litster, Angus and Sadie Lockhart, David Longley, John and Rhoda MacSween, Ian MacSween, Bev Margerison, Gina and Roger Martlew, Frank and Louise Moran, and Anne Ure.

Our especial thanks to Jean Williamson, who as well as providing the imaginative reconstructions and location map also assisted with most stages of the fieldwork, photography and design of the book; to Jim Killgore for all his encouragement and help, which included editing the final draft; and to our editor at Batsford, Peter Kemmis Betty.

# ONE

# INTRODUCTION

In May 1983 ploughing in a field on the Hebridean island of Rhum churned up a large scatter of tiny stone flakes, later identified as the debris from stone tool manufacture. A team of archaeologists headed by Caroline Wickham-Jones began excavations in the area in the following summer and uncovered traces of what proved to be the earliest known settlement in Scotland, occupied some 8500 years ago.

A series of pits, postholes and charcoal from hearth areas was uncovered, along with the probable floor outline of a tent. The site is thought to have been the temporary camp of a group of Mesolithic settlers, who lived by hunting deer and smaller animals, fishing and gathering nuts and fruits. These hunter-gatherers were some of the first people to inhabit Scotland after the final (Devensian) glaciation of the last ice age.

By the time the Rhum settlement was occupied, human groups had probably been living in Britain intermittently for at least 450,000 years. Evidence for the earliest Palaeolithic settlers is most often found in the south of England. The multipurpose pebble tools and hand-axes of these people have been recovered from river gravel terraces and the deposits of caves and rock shelters.

Occupation may have been more widespread than we have evidence for, extending into the north of England and Scotland. Subsequent periods of glaciation would have ground away any traces of this early settlement.

During the Devensian, ice sheets extended over much of Britain, covering most of Wales, the west Midlands, and the area to the north. Northern Britain was blanketed by a large expanse of ice which also stretched over much of northern Europe.

A drop in sea level accompanies glaciation, and the area which is now the North Sea was part of an arctic tundra environment stretching to the south of the ice sheets. The landscape was largely treeless, with low shrubs and mosses, and permanently frozen ground (permafrost). Animals suited to these conditions would have included woolly rhinoceros, mammoth, wolf,

bison and arctic bear. At the height of the Devensian from about 25,000 to 12,000 BC, 'Britain' was largely uninhabited, with average temperatures around −8°C.

The climate began to improve about 15,000 BC, leading to a period of mass extinctions perhaps aggravated by overhunting. Large mammals such as the mammoth and woolly rhinoceros eventually became extinct. Within 3000 years, the south of Britain was again suitable for habitation, and was slowly repopulated by groups following the herds of reindeer, horse, elk and red deer migrating from the warmer conditions of the south. Woodland began to regenerate in the south of England, mainly birch initially.

Between 11,000 and 10,000 BC the climate again deteriorated, and the ice sheets readvanced over the far north of Britain. It was not until after this period that woodland began to regenerate in Scotland.

By around 8000 BC much of present-day Britain was covered in woodland, which supported such animals as wild pig, ox, and red and roe deer. Among the stone flakes found at the site on Rhum were 'microliths', tiny stone blades which would have been hafted to a wooden shaft to form cutting edges, tips and barbs. Microlith-using groups are termed by archaeologists as Mesolithic, or Middle Stone Age, to differentiate them from the earlier Palaeolithic, Old Stone Age, groups.

As well as very different tool manufacture, the Mesolithic groups relied less on hunting and more on fishing and gathering nuts, fruits and shellfish than did their Palaeolithic predecessors. They could have operated from a stable base for most of the time, using seasonal camps within the area, rather than tracking the migrating herds as the Palaeolithic hunters would have done.

As the ice sheets melted, sea levels rose, accompanied by some isostatic uplift of the land as the weight of the overlying ice was removed. The land link with the area that is now Ireland had been severed by about 7000 BC, but Britain was still joined to the European mainland until about 6000 BC.

There is no record of domesticated plants and animals

*Memsie round cairn, Rathen, Banff and Buchan, the only survivor of a group of three Bronze Age cairns*

in Britain until the mid fourth millennium BC. It is thought that farming groups initially came to Britain from the Continent – there are earlier dates for domestication in parts of Europe, for example along the Rhine Valley.

The change to farming would not have been sudden. As domesticated plants (wheat and barley) and animals (cattle, sheep, goats and pigs) were adopted, hunting and gathering would still have played a big part in the subsistence. In many areas hunter-gatherers existed alongside groups relying mainly on farming, until around 3000 BC. Evidence for early farming settlement in Scotland is not much later than in southern England, and much of the early colonisation may have been by boat along the Irish Sea.

Keeping domesticated animals and cultivating crops necessitated a more sedentary life-style, and the predictable food supplies allowed time to be allotted to communal activities such as the building of chambered tombs. The term Neolithic (New Stone Age) is used to indicate these fundamental social changes, as well as changes in the material culture which included polished stone axes, querns and, for the first time, pottery.

Climatically temperatures continued to improve. By about 3000 BC they were similar to those of today, perhaps slightly warmer. Larger areas of woodland were cleared for fields, possibly by a combination of chopping and burning of dead wood. The northern parts of Scotland were probably treeless by about 3500 BC, with scrub and moorland replacing the forests, perhaps as much through natural selection as human activity.

During the third millennium BC another type of communal monument was being constructed in Scotland, the henge. Henges are circular areas enclosed by an interior ditch and exterior bank, sometimes with standing stones erected within. They may have been meeting places, for ceremonies or trade. Not all standing stones are within henges; unenclosed stone circles and standing stones are also found in many areas of Scotland.

Just as farming characterises the Neolithic, the emergence of metalworking marks the next division in Scottish prehistory: the Bronze Age. Like the preceding periods it is characterised by a major change in technology, but there were also far-reaching social changes.

Metallurgy was, like farming, most probably introduced into Britain from the Continent of Europe, around 2000 BC – though it is also thought that Ireland, with its large resources of copper, may have played an important role in the introduction of metalworking

*Strichen recumbent stone circle, Banff and Buchan, was uprooted by the tenant farmer in the late eighteenth century. He was forced by the landlord to re-erect the circle, which he did, although not in the same spot. The site was excavated in 1979–83, and the stones restored to their original positions*

into Scotland. Scottish copper axes are very similar to their Irish predecessors.

Along with the early metalwork, a type of pottery known as the beaker appeared. Beakers are finely made narrow pots, often richly decorated. Whether the pottery (found widely in Western Europe) represents an influx of people into Britain, or can be attributed to trade and exchange, is still a matter of debate. Beakers are often found as grave goods, associated with fine ornaments of shale, jet, gold and bronze.

The most usual grave form associated with beaker pottery is individual inhumation in a short cist, although cremations, sometimes in pottery urns, were also common in the early part of the Bronze Age. Round cairns were often built over the burials, but earlier monuments such as henges and chambered tombs were occasionally reused as burial sites by these later groups.

Metalworking necessitated the establishment of trade links for the procurement of raw materials. Unlike stone and flint, ores are concentrated in certain areas, and it is probable that local groups would have taken control of the resources once their value was realised. Whereas Neolithic communities were largely self-sufficient, control of the ore deposits allowed certain

*Overlooking the Kilphedir Burn in Sutherland are the remains of a broch. Although the broch is ruinous, the two surrounding ramparts and the deep ditch between them are still well preserved*

communities, and presumably individuals, to amass power and wealth.

Bronze Age settlements included stone and wood-built houses, and hut settlements. During the early first millennium BC there was a deterioration in the climate, with an increase in rainfall and a decrease in average temperatures. Peat began to form in upland areas, many of which were abandoned. This created population pressure and tensions. There is evidence in southern Scotland that some settlements were surrounded by a wooden palisade, and the increase in weapon types seems to back up this apparent concern with defence. Spearheads, axes and palstaves were among the weapons being cast.

In Scotland the Bronze Age ended in the middle of the first millennium BC, by which time swords and shields were also being manufactured. Trading

included not only raw materials but also the finished product. In Scotland, for example, beaten bronze vessels thought to have been made on the Continent have been found.

The next centuries saw a marked increase in the number of defended sites built in Scotland. The period is called the Iron Age, being characterised by the beginnings of ironworking. Known sites of the period range from large hillforts in the south of Scotland, to the smaller stone-built brochs and duns of the north and west and the loch-dwellings, or crannogs.

Trade contacts with the European mainland continued throughout the Iron Age. The large defended settlements of southern and eastern Scotland also imply complex local trade, as it is unlikely that food for such concentrations of population could have been supplied from the immediate area.

This was the general situation when Gnaeus Julius Agricola advanced with his Roman legions into southern Scotland in AD 80.

Palaeolithic, Mesolithic, Neolithic, Bronze Age and Iron Age: these, as we have seen, are the basic divisions

of Scottish prehistory which archaeologists use as their guidelines. They are convenient, but largely arbitrary. An average generation of people living in Scotland would not have been aware of much change, either environmentally or socially; most of the changes were very gradual.

Scottish prehistory has been studied since the middle of last century by many different people, with many different aims. Often in the past it was the most obvious structures, such as chambered tombs and round cairns which were the targets of 'investigations'. Many were dug into and emptied, with no records kept of the finds, much less their contexts. Today just as much emphasis is put on the more 'mundane' aspects of Scottish archaeology such as field systems, hut circles and burnt mounds, which provide a more balanced picture of prehistoric life.

Even with the detailed surveys possible today, it is difficult to reconstruct the prehistoric landscape accu-

*Two Bronze Age trough querns and moulers from the site of Jarlshof in Shetland (p. 32)*

*Detail of the 'kitchen midden' at Jarlshof in Shetland (p. 32), showing some of the thousands of limpet shells which are one of the midden's main components*

rately. The survival of sites does not necessarily represent the original distribution of the prehistoric population. Stone-built structures will generally survive better than those which were built of wood or turf. In areas where cultivable land extends over the upland areas, more sites will have been lost than in areas which are used mainly for grazing.

In recent years, the technology available to archaeologists has increased greatly. Aerial photography and geophysical survey are used to locate sites. In excavation, the use of computers can make the recording of a site much quicker. Pollen analysis is used to reconstruct the prehistoric environment. Dating methods such as Carbon 14 can help determine the age of sites more

accurately than the study of artefacts alone. Palaeopathology gives an indication of the physical appearance and diseases of the prehistoric communities.

Gathering and piecing together the information on life and society in prehistoric Scotland is still a slow process even with scientific techniques. Resources are limited and often have to be allocated to sites threatened with destruction, such as those on forestry land and in coastal areas, rather than to research projects. The following chapters present a selection of settlement, defensive, burial and ceremonial sites, some excavated, others not, all of which add to our understanding of Scotland's prehistory.

# TWO
# SETTLEMENT

An imaginative reconstruction of a crannog, based on information from various excavations and surveys. It shows wooden piles retaining an artificial mound of brushwood, a causeway and a landing stage (under construction).

Locating the settlement sites of Scotland's Mesolithic hunter-gatherers is not an easy task. Some groups would have been nomadic, following herds of deer and setting up camp as they went. As well as making use of natural shelters such as rock overhangs, they carried skin tents, which were pitched in sheltered spots. Little trace of these temporary encampments survive, and the most obvious remains of many early sites are flint scatters, signs of stone tool manufacture.

Other Mesolithic sites represent more permanent occupation. On Oronsay, for example, Mesolithic groups living along the shore left six shell mounds or 'middens', measuring up to 30m (100ft) in diameter and 3.5m (12ft) in height. The mounds date to the mid-fifth millennium BC and the amount of food represented suggests semi-permanent, perhaps seasonal, occupation. Bone harpoon-heads and fish-hooks were among the implements recorded during excavations, most recently by Paul Mellars. All the evidence indicated a heavy reliance on seafood.

Farming in Neolithic times necessitated greater permanency, and the early farmers lived either in farmsteads occupied by one or two families, or in small communities such as at Rinyo (Rousay), Noltland (Westray) and Scotland's most famous Neolithic settlement site, Skara Brae on Orkney Mainland (p. 25). In Shetland, houses with attached fields as at Ness of Gruting (p. 29) and Scord of Brouster (p. 29) have also been ascribed a Neolithic date.

In areas where timber was used for building, little trace remains of these farmsteads. Even in areas such as Orkney where stone was used, important sites are often well hidden. At Pool on Sanday, Orkney – the Neolithic and later settlement recently excavated by John Hunter was recognised only after coastal erosion had exposed buildings and midden deposits in the cliff section.

Settlement in the Bronze Age is also enigmatic, though survey and excavation are gradually beginning to fill in the gaps. Excavations at Tofts Ness, also on Sanday, by Steve Dockerill have, for example, uncovered remains of round-houses dating from the late Neolithic through to the Bronze Age.

Evidence for circular timber houses has been found throughout Scotland including Muirkirk in Ayrshire, while in other areas the numerous hut circles and field systems which are being recorded by survey, for example in Perthshire, may on excavation give a Bronze Age date.

The later Bronze Age marks the beginning of a trend to enclose settlements, which continues in the Iron Age.

Apart from defended settlements (discussed in the next chapter) unenclosed settlements are still found in the Iron Age. These include wheelhouses as at Jarlshof (p. 32), crannogs (lake dwellings) and souterrains (underground buildings) such as Grain (p. 44), which were probably storehouses attached to settlements above ground.

Farming probably changed little from the Neolithic to the Iron Age. Apart from sheep, goats, pigs and cattle, dogs were also domesticated at an early stage, and there is evidence that they were used by hunters even before the beginning of farming. Dogs may have been a source of food, though this is improbable, as often complete skeletons are found. Horses may have been domesticated by the early Bronze Age, but perhaps as a food source as no equestrian equipment is found before the late Bronze Age.

Just which animals were raised probably depended on available grazing. At Northton in Harris, there were equal numbers of cattle and sheep, but no pigs, perhaps because of lack of woodland. Evidence from numerous sites has shown that these early domesticates were much smaller than modern breeds.

Wild animals became less important in the diet as time went on, but in some areas much of the meat still came from hunting. At the Iron Age site of Dun Ardtreck in Skye (p. 70), red deer represented 24 per cent of the animals identified.

Cattle were kept for milking, as well as for a stable meat supply. At Skara Brae among other sites it has been noted that many of the calves were slaughtered. This has often been attributed to a lack of sufficient fodder for over-wintering, but equally it may be consistent with dairying. In coastal areas at least, seaweed could have been used as winter fodder.

Crop cultivation is often more difficult to trace. Sometimes it is only indirect evidence such as sickles and querns which survive, but at some sites conditions are right for the survival of carbonised seeds and plants. Grain impressions have been found in pottery, where a seed or grain has been caught up in the clay during the forming of a pot, and subsequently burnt out.

Naked and six-row barley and emmer wheat were the main crops grown by Neolithic farmers in Britain. In the northern and upland sites of Scotland, barley was most suitable.

Such a mixed economy of crops and animals necessitated enclosed fields to stop the crops being trampled. Animals were penned at night to protect them from predators.

Pollen studies show a marked decline in tree pollen in the Neolithic. This is probably due, at least in part, to the clearance of woodland for fields. Stones also had to be cleared before planting could take place, and in many areas 'clearance cairns' are found near the boundaries of early cultivation. Ploughing was probably with an ard.

Wild plants, fruits and nuts were gathered to supplement the diet, while fish and shellfish remained important resources at coastal sites. Wild birds and small mammals were also caught and eaten.

In addition to the seasonal farming and hunting duties, a great deal of time was spent in making clothing, utensils, weapons, and tools.

Flint is found in many areas of Scotland, mainly in glacial deposits or along the coast. Arrowheads, knives, axes and other sharp-edged tools were fashioned by flaking and retouching. In areas where flint was not available, other fine-grained rocks were worked in much the same way.

Larger stone implements, such as hammerstones and ards, were made out of whatever stone was available locally, and techniques of manufacture were adapted to suit the material.

Pottery is one of the main finds on excavations of Neolithic date and later, and was used for cooking and storage. Despite the dominance of clay vessels, it is certain that other containers of basketry, leather and wood were also used, but these decay quickly unless a site is waterlogged.

Pottery vessels were hand-built – the wheel was not introduced until the late Iron Age – and could have been fired on the domestic hearth. Ceramics are often

*Clettraval wheelhouse settlement, Tigharry, North Uist, looking west at the house which is built into the body of a chambered tomb*

distinctive in shape and decoration and in many cases are good chronological indicators.

Many implements such as pins, awls and combs were made from bone and antler. Sturdy red deer antlers were often used to make more heavy-duty tools such as picks.

Metal working required more equipment, know-how and the ability to obtain the raw materials. Scotland has resources of copper and gold, but no tin, which presumably had to be brought from Cornwall or the Continent. Copper could have been cold hammered or cast in open molds, but bronze smelting needed more carefully controlled conditions for the successful combination of the metals.

Wool-processing and weaving was also a common activity on prehistoric sites, as was the working of animal skins and furs to make clothing. Typical garments may have been a type of trouser and tunic, or a single wrapped tunic, with capes and shawls for extra warmth in the winter months. Skin or fur clothes can be fastened by toggles, whereas pins are better for use with tunics. Often these fastenings were decorative – jet buttons have survived, as have decorated bronze and bone pins.

Some objects were purely ornamental. Shell and bone necklaces, as well as those of amber and jet, have been found in Neolithic and early Bronze Age sites in Scotland. Gold earrings (only from a cist at Orbliston, Morayshire) and lunulae have been recovered – these belong to the early Bronze Age. Some weapons were so finely made and decorated that it is hard to believe they were ever used in combat – these too may have been personal ornaments.

Transport before the invention of the wheel (introduced into Britain in the late Bronze Age) was by sled or, where possible, by boat. Remains of dug-out canoes have been discovered in waterlogged sites, and it is likely that wood-framed, skin-covered corracles were also used for fishing or travelling. Even when the wheel

*The interior of Laid souterrain, Sutherland, looking along the curved passage towards the stepped entrance*

was introduced, sleds were more effective for crossing the rough terrain in most areas of Scotland.

No matter how many sites are excavated, some aspects of life in prehistoric Scotland can never be known – games played, music and songs, language and legend. But we known that life was not without some pleasures, even an occasional 'dram'. Fibrous material adhering to pottery sherds from the Neolithic levels at Kinloch on Rhum, was interpreted by archaeobotanist, Brian Moffit, as being the residue of an ale or mead, Scotland's earliest known alcohol.

# KNAP OF HOWAR

Five and a half thousand years ago, the outlook from the farmstead known as Knap of Howar, on the Orkney island of Papa Westray, would have been very different from today. Instead of being buffeted by coastal gales, environmental evidence from the site indicates that the buildings stood in open grassland behind a line of sand dunes. It is also possible that Papa Westray was joined to the larger island of Westray during the Neolithic, the period in which the farmstead was occupied.

*The smaller of the two houses at Knap of Howar, showing its division into three compartments, with the hearth and quern in the central one. In the far left corner is the door connecting it with its larger neighbour*

The site was first excavated in the 1930s by William Traill, and William Kirkness. Further excavations were carried out in 1973 by Anna Ritchie.

From the excavations something of the life of the people who inhabited the buildings can be established. Two rectilinear structures were built side by side. Both had good drystone walling, constructed with two faces, a core of midden material between. The larger building was entered along a passage, paved and roofed with slabs. At the inner end more slabs formed door checks and jambs.

Inside, the 10 by 5m (33 by 16ft) living space was divided by stone slabs into two rooms. The room nearest the door was the larger and had a low bench along one wall; it was probably used as the main living

area. On the floor of the inner room were stone 'footings' which may have supported wooden benches. A central hearth and a large stone quern imply that this room was used for food preparation and cooking.

A connecting passage linked this house to the adjacent building, a slightly smaller structure also divided by stone partitions, in this case into three compartments. There was a hearth in the middle compartment, and several recesses were built into the wall of the inner compartment suggesting it may have been a store-room.

As to the roofing of the houses, traces of wooden posts indicate a hipped roof with timber rafters, rather than a slab-constructed roof.

Anna Ritchie has suggested that the two buildings were the home of one farming family. The smaller one may have been a workshop and store, while the larger provided the main living and sleeping space.

Knap of Howar was occupied during two separate periods, the earliest being prior to the building of the houses and represented by a thick accumulation of household rubbish. The houses themselves were built on this layer of 'midden'. At some point the smaller building went out of use – possibly because of wall collapse – and its entrance was sealed up.

A great deal of pottery was found at the site – coarse cooking wares and finer, well-decorated 'Unstan' bowls. There were bone awls and knives, a selection of flints and an implement that looked like a whalebone hoe. None of the artefacts were made from any material which could not have been obtained locally.

The inhabitants of the Knap of Howar were farmers, hunters and fishermen, as well as skilled craftsmen. Although the soil conditions were poor for the preservation of organics, a few barley grains were recovered, and wheat pollen was identified. Domestic animals reared by the inhabitants were mainly sheep and cattle, but there were also some pigs. Bones from such birds as puffin and guillemot were found – they may have been trapped to extract their oil for use in lamps. The fish caught included both inshore varieties such as saithe and rockling and also deepwater fish like cod and ling. Shellfish (limpets, razor, winkles and cockles) were also collected.

Apart from being one of the oldest known buildings in Orkney, Knap of Howar is also important for its Unstan ware. Previous to the excavations at the site it was thought that these decorated shallow bowls were used exclusively as funerary pottery, and that grooved ware was everyday pottery. It now seems that this was due to a lack of excavation of settlement sites. The current thinking is that there is a chronological difference between grooved ware and Unstan ware, the Unstan ware being earlier, but with makers of both grooved ware and Unstan ware coexisting in the Orkneys for some time.

# SKARA BRAE

In 1850 a great storm pounded the shore of the Bay of Skaill, on Orkney Mainland, leaving the buildings of a Neolithic settlement sticking up through the sand dunes which had covered them.

The first systematic excavations of the site at Skara Brae were carried out by V.G. Childe in 1927. After removing about half a metre of sand, the archaeological levels were reached. Between the buildings, excavators found 'midden' material full of shells and bones, pieces of pottery and discarded stone and bone tools – the household rubbish of several centuries. This compacted material was presumably used for insulation.

*The interior of House 7 of Skara Brae, showing the slab-built dresser, the central hearth with a stone bench beside it, and the beds against the walls*

Skara Brae's occupants were farmers who bred cows and sheep and grew cereals, but also hunted red deer and fished. They were skilled craftsmen, working bone and stone, and making pottery. Many of the tools, weapons and vessels, even stones set into the house walls, were richly decorated, and it is possible that they decorated their bodies as well – small containers which had held red ochre were found during the excavations.

Originally Skara Brae was set back from the shore – coastal erosion now threatens the site. The village was planned as a cluster of sub-rectangular huts, with interconnecting passages. Seven connected houses were uncovered during Childe's excavations. Their walls were made of sandstone slabs, most laid in courses. Corbelled walling probably formed the roofs, but whale jawbones were discovered on the floor of one

*One of the flagged passages of the settlement. On the left where the passage narrows is the entrance to House 1*

hut, perhaps originally used as rafters to support a thatched roof. Only one house had a window – in the rest the door was the only opening.

All the houses had a similar interior design. Against the wall facing the door was the dresser – a couple of flag-stone shelves supported on stone 'legs'. This may have been the display case for the family's prized possessions, carefully positioned to impress visitors. In the centre of each hut was a rectangular hearth edged by four kerbstones. Along each of the two side walls was a bed, constructed of three slabs set upright to form a 'box', the house wall forming the fourth side. Heather or straw would have been piled inside these beds to form a springy 'mattress'. Above the beds were recesses

in the walls, perhaps storage places for personal belongings.

A common feature of the hut interiors is a 'limpet box', a slab-built tank made watertight by clay luting and sometimes set into the floor. David Clarke who excavated areas of the remaining middens in the early 1970s suggested that limpets were stored in these boxes as fish bait, especially in the winter when other bait was more difficult to find. Limpets can be used as bait if they are soaked for about a week to soften them.

Set apart from the connecting huts was an open paved area which Childe called the Market Place, and a separate hut, without furniture, possibly a workshop.

Just why Skara Brae was abandoned is a mystery.

*The flag-stone jambs and bar-holes of the entrance to House 1 at Skara Brae, looking from the interior of the house*

*A detail of the interior of House 7, looking at one of the beds with various 'keeping places' above it*

Excavation evidence seems to indicate that the village's occupants left in a hurry, perhaps fleeing from a storm similar to the one which uncovered the site. Decorated grooved ware vessels still stood on the hut floors, and other objects such as bone pins were scattered about. A broken necklace left a trail of beads along one passage.

# STANYDALE

The late Neolithic site of Stanydale on Shetland Mainland is best known for its so-called 'temple', a large building with walls 4m (13ft) thick. Six alcoves were built into the wall of the 12 by 6.5m (39 × 22ft) round chamber, in the arc opposite the door. Two central postholes contained timbers supporting a ridge pole for the roof.

The finds from the 'temple' – stone tools and pottery – provide few clues to its function, but the structure is certainly much larger than the surrounding houses, and was probably some kind of communal meeting place.

*One of the excavated houses which can be found in the area around the Stanydale 'temple'*

*The Stanydale 'temple' with its entrance passage in the foreground and the alcoves in the opposite wall. The stones in the central area mark the positions of the postholes*

# GRUTING AND SCORD OF BROUSTER

In the area around the 'temple' at Stanydale in Shetland (p. 28) are the outlines of several clusters of houses. One such group is near the shore of Scutta Voe, about a kilometre from Stanydale. Here are the remains of three houses. The road to Gruting School has cut through one, and a garage has been built on another. The third was excavated just after the Stanydale site when C.S.T. Calder noticed that it was being destroyed by some schoolboys imitating his work at the 'temple'.

The excavated house was oval in shape, with two chambers, the larger measuring 7.5 by 5.5m (25 by 18ft) and the smaller one only 3m (10ft) in diameter. In each chamber there was a recess containing a roughly built stone bench. The house probably had a thatched roof with wooden rafters.

There were signs that the house had been occupied on more than one occasion. No well-dated artefacts were found – most were roughly made stone tools. The pottery was identified as 'Neolithic and later'.

In the vicinity were 'clearance cairns', piles of stones left at the side of a field when the area was cleared for cultivation. Bone fragments from similar houses nearby were identified as horse, ox and sheep, suggesting a mixed economy of cultivation and husbandry.

*The excavated house near Gruting School, overlooking the shore of Scutta Voe*

On a rock strewn Shetland hillside, barely covered by peat, is one of the most complete Neolithic settlements in Scotland, Scord of Brouster. Houses, clearance cairns and enclosures dot the slope. Excavations were carried out by Alasdair Whittle in the 1970s.

The settlement comprises three oval houses, each within its own field. There are traces of other fields delineated by stone walls or banks, and the maximum extent of the enclosed area is about five acres. Beyond this site are the remains of numerous other fields and houses. Radiocarbon dates indicate that the site was inhabited from the late third millennium to the early second millennium BC in its main phase of occupation.

Two of the houses are directly connected to the surrounding field walls. The largest house (House 1) measures 7 by 5m (23 by 16ft) internally, with a 1–2m (3–6ft) thick wall, the interior of which was faced. Four large pillars jutting out from the wall divided the main living area. In the centre was a hearth.

House 2, the other house built against a field wall, had a kidney-shaped interior projecting pillars forming two recesses. No hearth was uncovered. The third house was built in the same way, and had a central hearth.

Carbonised barley was found in each house, and this along with 'weeds of cultivation' identified from pollen studies and the recovery of stone ard points and mattock heads suggests that the fields around the houses were used for crop-growing. The bones of sheep and cattle were also found. The animals may have been grazed in the fields after the harvest. The settlement is on ground that would be considered unsuitable for cultivation now, though before the apparent climatic deterioration in the Bronze Age (with its associated peat growth) the land was probably quite fertile.

*Scord of Brouster settlement, looking at one of the fields with its clearance cairns and a house in the top right corner*

# PETTIGARTHS FIELD

On the island of Whalsay, Shetland, in an area called Pettigarths Field, are four archaeological sites. Two are burial sites (a chambered cairn and a cist). The others, 'The Standing Stones of Yoxie' and the 'Benie Hoose', were interpreted by the excavator, C.S.T. Calder, as the remains of a 'temple' and a house. It is now thought that both are examples of prehistoric houses.

The houses are of similar design, with a passage leading into the house from a courtyard. The Standing Stones of Yoxie is two-roomed, whereas the Benie Hoose is one-roomed, and the rooms were further partitioned by recesses or alcoves. The excavation evidence suggested that the houses were first occupied during the Neolithic.

Finds from both sites included pottery, hammer-stones, pounders, stone axes, and stone picks. Although 33 quern-stones were found at the Benie Hoose, none were found at Yoxie, part of the reasoning behind assigning it the status of a temple rather than a house.

The chambered tomb was probably used by the occupants of the houses although direct evidence is missing – it had been opened prior to excavation, and the finds removed.

*The Benie Hoose with the courtyard in the foreground, and the remains of the passage leading into the house*

# LIDDLE

Near Liddle farmhouse on South Ronaldsay, Orkney is a burnt mound, one of very few to have been excavated, although over 400 have been recorded in Orkney and Shetland.

Before excavation a burnt mound usually looks like a heap of fire-cracked stones. Liddle was no exception. The mound, which was about 2m (6ft) high, was made up of a mixture of burnt stones, ash (mainly from peat) and carbon. In the centre, however, a building was discovered, oval in shape and with dimensions of 6.5 by 4m (21 by 13ft). The floor was flagged, and a hearth had been set into a cavity in the wall. In the centre of the building was a large trough made of flagstones.

The purpose of burnt mounds is uncertain. In excavated examples, a trough big enough to hold up to 1000 litres of water is common, and the sites are usually found near a fresh water source. Combined with traces of large fires found in or around the sites, the most logical solution is that they were cooking places.

An alternative to cooking in a large pottery vessel over a fire was to bring water to the boil in a trough by the addition of hot stones, add the food, and then maintain the temperature by adding more stones until cooking was complete. Baking could have been carried out by digging a hole, heating it with hot stones, adding

*Liddle burnt mound after excavation, showing the central tank, housed within a stone-built shelter*

the wrapped food, and then sealing the 'oven' until the food was cooked. Substantial amounts of burnt stones would have accumulated if these practices were consistently repeated.

Another, though less likely, suggestion is that the burnt mounds were the remains of saunas, perhaps used for 'ritual purification'.

# JARLSHOF

Jarlshof, in the southern part of mainland Shetland not far from Sumburgh airport, is a complex site, its occupation spanning from the Bronze Age to the seventeenth century. The final occupancy is represented by the early seventeenth-century laird's house, built over part of a broch. The house was known as Sumburgh, until it was renamed 'Jarlshof' by Sir Walter Scott in *The Pirate*, and the name has been used since.

Among the earliest structures on the site were Bronze Age stone built circular and oval houses with projecting walls dividing the interior. To call these 'houses' is not quite correct, as there is evidence that their use changed over the life of the settlement. One was used as a byre. A whale-vertebra ring was set into the wall, presumably for tethering, and the floor, which sloped to a central sump, suggests the draining of manure.

Another house was used by a smith for part of the time, as a workshop. Many pieces of clay moulds were found during the excavations, including those for swords and socketed axes. In addition to metal, stone was also used for the manufacture of axes. Pottery vessels were manufactured, and small bowls were carved from steatite (soapstone). Bones from the midden associated with the settlement indicate that cattle, sheep and pigs were kept.

*Part of the multi-period settlement at Jarlshof, with a later Iron Age wheelhouse superimposed over a Bronze Age house, and the entrance to a souterrain in the middle*

*The interior of Wheelhouse 1 at Jarlshof. The radiating piers provide compartments which are further divided by slabs set on end. There is a central stone-lined hearth*

The site was abandoned for a while after the Bronze Age and covered over by wind-blown sand. A broch surrounded by a courtyard was later built on the site, in the Iron Age. An aisled round house with a large rectangular stone hearth in the centre was subsequently constructed in one end of the enclosure. Sometime around the middle of the first millennium AD, two wheelhouses were built from the stones of the aisled round house.

Wheelhouses and aisled round houses are related forms of architecture. In wheelhouses, stone piers radiate from the side of a stone-built round house, like the spokes of a wheel. The piers would have had two functions – to support the roof, and also to partition off different areas of the house interior. The remaining central area was often dominated by a hearth. With aisled round houses, the piers are not attached to the house walls, but are free-standing, leaving a clear aisle around the inside perimeter of the house wall.

These 'post-broch' Iron Age houses were succeeded some centuries later by an extensive settlement of rectangular houses built by Norse settlers.

# CORBURY HILL AND NORMANGILL RIG

On opposite sides of the Midlock Water in Clydesdale lie two unenclosed platform settlements, Corbury Hill and Normangill Rig. Many similar sites are to be found in the area, Normangill Rig being the largest.

   The platforms are all that remain of settlements of late Bronze Age timber houses. Before putting up the timber frame of a house, a scoop was dug out of the hillside and spread out to form a level area of ground. At Normangill Rig the platforms measure 11–21m (36—68ft) in diameter.

*One of the hut platforms of the unenclosed settlement of Normangill Rig, across the valley from Corbury Hill*

*Above a cutbank on a bend of the Midlock Water are the platforms representing the levelled sites of at least five Bronze Age timber houses*

# RITCHIE FERRY

Along a ridge at the foot of Ritchie Ferry in Clydesdale are the outlines of a settlement, two small enclosures and a homestead. The sites have not been excavated, but from comparison with other excavated sites, their occupation probably dates to the later first millennium BC and the early first millennium AD.

The largest of the sites is the settlement, which comprised a group of about eight round timber houses surrounded by a bank of earth and stone. There were four entrances into the enclosure, one at each side, which suggests that defence was not a major consideration. Although the bank looks somewhat like a rampart, it has been built by scraping up earth and stone from either side, rather than by digging a ditch to provide material for a massive defence. The idea for ramparts may eventually have come about from the enlargement of banks such as these.

Five of the houses inside are similar to those found at the unenclosed platform settlements of Corbury Hill and Normangill Rig (p. 34). The other three have been built by a different method. They are ring-ditch houses in which posts for the house walls were set in an unbroken bedding trench.

To the west of the settlement is the 'homestead', an oval enclosure and hut platform surrounded by a stone wall, and to the east side of the settlement are the remains of two further enclosures.

*The settlement of Ritchie Ferry, its earthen bank surrounding the knoll just above the track. To the left is the outline of one of the smaller enclosures*

# NEW KINORD

The New Kinord hut circles and enclosures, near Ballater, Kincardine and Deeside, were among those prehistoric sites carefully recorded by Sir Alexander Ogston. Sir Alexander was physician to Queen Victoria, and a medical researcher, but in his scarce free time he enjoyed studying the prehistoric remains found near his estate, Glendavan. On his death the typescript, maps, plans and photographs for a book on the archaeology of the area were found.

The hut circles at New Kinord are found close to some birch woods, clustered round the bottom of a rounded hillock which to some extent determines the settlement's shape.

Stretches of walling form a triangular-shaped enclosure which surrounds the settlement. Circular stone outlines within the enclosure are all that remain of the various hut circles or houses. The largest is 19m (62ft) in diameter, slightly sunk into the ground, with very thick walling. There are traces of a souterrain with entrances into one if not two of the huts.

Without excavation it is often difficult to tell the age of such sites, but it is thought that the settlement belongs to the late first millennium BC.

Not far from New Kinord is a second settlement – Old Kinord – which has a similar cluster of huts within a stone walled enclosure.

*Part of the New Kinord settlement, looking from the wall of the largest house towards an adjacent circular enclosure*

# KILPHEDIR

Scattered over the north of Scotland are many examples of 'hut circles', ring-like banks of stones about 5–12m (16–40ft) in diameter. It is thought that they are the remains of stone foundations of round houses. In Sutherland alone there may be as many as 2000 hut circles. Despite their numbers, few have been excavated. One of the sites which has undergone excavation is a group of five hut circles overlooking Kilphedir Burn in the Strath of Kildonan. They were built on the slope of a hill – a typical setting – probably to overcome drainage problems.

Evidence from the excavations at Kilphedir suggests that the huts were occupied in the late Bronze Age and early Iron Age, probably by a succession of families. In the interior of one hut, a ring of postholes was found which could have supported the rafters of a conical roof. The other end of the rafters would have rested on the foundation. As there was no central posthole, it is most likely that the rafters were secured together at the apex, like a tepee top.

Hearths were excavated within the huts, and pieces of pottery, quern stones, stone pounders and flint tools were typical of the artefacts recovered.

*The largest of a group of hut circles in the Strath of Kildonan. A souterrain runs under the hut wall on the left side*

# CRANNOGS

Crannogs, or lake dwellings, are small islets, at least partly man-made, on which stone or wooden homesteads were built. Some crannogs, such as Milton Loch, Stewarty were connected to the shore by a causeway. C.M. Piggott, who excavated Milton Loch crannog in 1953, concluded that it had been the home of a farming family. A farming connection is also supported by a survey of crannogs in Loch Awe, Argyll, which suggested that they were deliberately sited with good land on the adjacent shore.

Many crannogs are still prominent features of the Scottish landscape, while others are either wholly or partially submerged, and best spotted from the air. Some probably date back to the late Bronze Age, and there is documentation of their use up to the seventeenth century. Their design and siting suggest a need for defence, perhaps for the protection of animals and food stocks from wild animals or aggressive neighbours.

Crannog builders were skilled in choosing suitable locations as well as in construction. The best sites needed little additional building, making full use of natural features. To pinpoint these sites, an area would have been 'surveyed' with a pole or a weighted line, implying the use of boats, probably skin-covered corracles or dug-out canoes. When a site was chosen, it was built up, often using layers of wood and stones, with vertical piles for added strength where necessary.

Interest in Scottish crannogs began in the mid nineteenth century. Robert Munro pioneered the research in Scotland, publishing his *Ancient Scottish Lake Dwellings or Crannogs*, in 1882. He excavated a number of sites including Lochlee in Ayrshire.

Early underwater exploration was not easy. In 1908 Rev. Odo Blundell used a diving suit borrowed from the Caledonian Canal divers to explore the crannog of Eilean Muireach in Loch Ness. His report of the day's events states:

> The first descent was made in about 12 feet of water on the west side of the island, but, owing to the inexperience of the amateurs at the air pump, little serious work was done. The excess of air which was supplied to me had the effect of making me so buoyant that I was floating over the top of the stones instead of stepping firmly on them, and that despite the two lead weights of 56 lbs each attached to the already very heavy helmet and boots.

Nowadays, methods of underwater exploration are much more refined, the aim being to achieve standards similar to land-based excavations, in terms of surveying, excavating and recording and recovering finds. Crannog excavations are important because artefacts seldom surviving underground, such as wood and leather, are often well preserved in the anaerobic conditions of a loch bottom.

---

*Ardanaiseig crannog, Loch Awe is set in the mouth of a little inlet, less than 100m from the shore. It has a cairn-shaped profile and is now overgrown with trees*

# WAG OF FORSE

In hilly country near Latheron in Caithness are the remains of a broch and surrounding settlement. From the distance the site appears to be a jumble of stone rubble, but closer up, the outlines of buildings become clear.

The site was occupied by various groups during the later first millennium BC and the early part of the first millennium AD. A cluster of stone huts were the earliest buidings on the site. Later a broch was built, the stones of which were eventually reused to build a series of pillared rectangular houses known as 'wags'.

One wag, to the west of the broch, is 12m (40ft) long. Within it are the remains of two rows of stone pillars which would have supported lintel stones. Flagstones and perhaps turf could have been placed on top to complete the roofing.

It was the excavator, A.O. Curle's opinion that the wags were unroofed cattle shelters rather than domestic sites. He postulated that the animals were coralled every night for protection and suggested that a fire would have been lit in one end after dark to frighten off any predators.

*One of the rectangular 'wags' at Forse, showing the remains of the rows of pillar stones, with one lintel in place*

# ARDESTIE

In February 1949 a farmer at Ardestie in Angus was carrying out stone-clearing operations in an especially stony field. As he worked, he found that some of the larger stones seemed to form the outline of a circle.

He reported his findings, and excavations lasting over a year were carried out by F.T. Wainwright. The remains at Ardestie consisted of a large curved souterrain, or earth-house, with four hut foundations at ground level.

The souterrain was constructed in a similar way to many others in the south east of Scotland. First a trench was dug into the boulder clay, then stone walls were built up inside the trench, the space between the wall and the trench side being carefully packed as building progressed. Rough paving covered the souterrain floor.

The roof of the Ardestie souterrain protruded above ground, especially towards the end of the passage, where the souterrain builders had run into a rock outcrop, and had to slope the tunnel upwards.

There were two entrances to the souterrain, one of which opened into one of the huts.

The souterrain fell into disuse at some point, and was dismantled, although settlement continued at ground level. The occupants appeared to have had trouble with drainage. Water which ran into the souterrain could not drain away through the boulder clay. An attempt was made to rectify this problem by taking up the paving of

*The banana-shaped souterrain of Ardestie with the position of the drain marked out. On ground level within the curve are the remains of the associated settlement*

the passage floor and building a drain below it, but this seems to have been unsuccessful.

The function of the souterrain is uncertain, but Wainwright was confident from its layout that it had been used as a cattle shelter. A subsidiary entrance was half-blocked by large boulders, presumably to keep animals in while also allowing for their observation. From the finds, the site was occupied between AD 150 and AD 450.

# BARNS OF AIRLIE

The souterrain on the farm of Barns of Airlie in Forfarshire was discovered in 1794 by a ploughman. Ploughing operations in one of the fields were constantly coming to a halt because of stones becoming caught up in the ploughs. One day 'just at the close of the forenoon yokin'' a stone larger than usual was struck. The ploughman stuck an iron lever into the edge of the stone and went off for his lunch. When he returned he brought the farmer to help him. To their surprise, the lever had disappeared, and on lifting the stone they uncovered a souterrain. It has not been totally excavated, and is at present 19m (62ft) long. One of the roof lintels is decorated with some cupmarks and serpent-like grooves.

This was the second souterrain found at Barns of Airlie. A story connected to the discovery of the first one relates that a cottar's wife could not understand why there were never any ashes left in her hearth, and why any small objects dropped near the fire just seemed to disappear. The final straw was when a bannock that she was making fell off the toaster and vanished. Believing the house was bewitched, she called the neighbours who pulled down the house. When this was done, one boy noticed a long crack in the hearth, and on lifting the flagstone discovered the explanation – a souterrain.

*The curving passage of Barns of Airlie souterrain with the carved lintel in the foreground. The present access is via an open section of the roof*

# CARLUNGIE

While excavating at Ardestie (p. 41), Wainwright was called to the nearby farm of Carlungie where the farmer had discovered an 'underground wall' while moving a large slab caught in his plough. This proved to be a souterrain. A second souterrain was found in the same field a month later.

The first site, Carlungie I, was excavated by Wainwright once he had finished at Ardestie. The souterrain was 'hook-shaped' and over 40m (130ft) long.

Above the souterrain was a settlement of eight huts, seven of which were set round a paved courtyard. The main entrance to the souterrain was off this courtyard, and there were three other entrances, one of which led off a semi-subterranean workshop. Another led to a passage which wound for 13m (44ft) before reaching the souterrain itself.

As at Ardestie, the Carlungie I souterrain had gone out of use before the settlement was abandoned. As it was dug into well-drained coarse sands and gravels, it is unlikely that flooding would have been a problem, but there was evidence that part of the roof had collapsed, and this may have led to its disuse.

Wainwright again believed that animals were kept in the souterrain. Tests carried out on soil in areas of the souterrain that would have been suitable for penning cattle, showed higher than normal nitrogen levels, thought to have derived from manure.

*Carlungie I souterrain, with its paved floor and large boulder foundation stones. Originally it would have been roofed above ground level*

# GRAIN

The earth-house at Grain in Kirkwall, Orkney, was first discovered in 1827. It was closed on discovery, and not opened again until it was excavated in 1857.

Unfortunately the records of the excavation are not very detailed, but we know that a large pit was excavated in the ground above the chamber. It was full of ash and charcoal, and had probably been a hearth. Animal bones and shells were found in quantity. All this suggests that the earth house had been part of large settlement on ground level.

The structure itself was well preserved, mainly because it was built so deep below the surface – there were two metres of earth between the roof and ground level. A flight of steps led down to the sloped passage which was over 4.5m (15ft) long and curved towards a bean-shaped chamber. Roofing slabs spanned the passage at a height of 1.5m (5ft).

The chamber roof was similar to that of the passage, and as at Rennibister (p. 46), was supported by four stone pillars. Where the pillars were not high enough, they were built up by placing 'eke' stones on the top.

Below *The curving passage of Grain earth-house, with its lintelled roof. At the far end are the stairs leading up to ground level*

Right *The four free-standing pillars in the chamber at Grain, with 'eke' stones extending the height of some*

# RENNIBISTER

Near Kirkwall on Orkney Mainland is Rennibister Farm, a distinctive Orkney farmhouse with large outbuildings. At this farm, on the 12 November 1926, a steam thresher was trundling out of the farm gate when the ground subsided beneath its wheels, and it became stuck in a large hole.

Help soon came from Kirkwall, and with considerable difficulty the thresher was pulled out. The cause of the trouble was found to be the roof of a souterrain, which had given way under the heavy weight of the machinery.

The earth-house was examined soon after. First the passage had to be cleared, the first few metres of which were blocked with domestic rubbish – black earth mixed with various shells. The rest of the passage and the chamber were clear, apart from the bottom of the chamber being water-logged.

The chamber was oval, measuring only 3.5 by 2.5m (12 by 8ft) with five recesses built into the walls. Its corbelled roof was supported by four freestanding slab pillars. Now the roof has a hatch and a ladder allowing entry to the chamber.

Inside the chamber were human bones representing the incomplete remains of six adults and twelve or thirteen adolescents. It is unusual to find human remains in an earth-house, and its is probable that use as a burial vault was the structure's secondary function.

*Part of the chamber at Rennibister, looking up the sloping passage to the original entrance. In the foreground are two of the pillars which support the roof*

# THREE
# DEFENCE

Imaginative reconstruction of Cademuir Hillfort. A 'chevaux de frise' extends along the inner edge of the rampart.

The reconstruction shows Celts shouting abuse at the opposition in the hope of provoking single combat. The clothes and weapons are based on finds from southern Scotland, and details from carvings from other areas.

Defended settlements were probably being built in Scotland as early as the late Neolithic. Recent excavations at Meldon Bridge in Tweeddale uncovered postholes which had held a strong timber palisade cutting off a promontory between two rivers. The site may have been ceremonial rather than defensive, however. In the interior, were traces of many pits, some of which held cremations. The remains of only one timber house were uncovered.

With the exception of Meldon Bridge, the earliest known fortified sites in Scotland, timber-laced forts, date from the mid-first millennium BC. At these forts, wooden beams supported either a stone wall or earthen rampart, as at Finavon, Angus (p. 84). Here the fort had burnt down and the fire was so intense that the rampart material had vitrified. Timber-laced forts are found mainly in central and eastern Scotland, and it is possible that some of these sites existed as unenclosed settlements before the building of the ramparts.

The main drawback with timber-laced ramparts was the difficulty of replacing rotten or fire-damaged timbers. To do this, the wall had to be taken apart. Many timber-laced forts, for example Woden Law, Roxburgh (p. 87), were later converted into 'multivallate' forts by the addition of one or more sets of earthen ramparts and ditches around the original defences.

Hilltop forts first appear in large numbers in the Iron Age, and have their largest concentration in the southeast of Scotland. Many are thought to have been occupied on a permanent basis, housing sizeable communities. In addition to the rampart-defended settlements, there were others defended by palisades. In some cases the palisaded settlement was later developed into a full-scale hillfort, as at Burnswark, Annandale and Eskdale (p. 90).

Whereas many of the hillforts in the south and east of Scotland had earthen ramparts, or were at least partly constructed of timber, the dominant building material of the northern and western defended sites, brochs and duns, was stone.

Brochs are unique to Scotland. They were stone-built round towers, with staircases that wound upwards between galleried walls and led to upper storeys and the wallhead. Some brochs reached impressive heights – the broch of Mousa in Shetland (p. 56) is still over 13m (43ft) in height.

There has been some disagreement by researchers as to whether brochs were occupied permanently, or only in times of danger. Excavation finds seem to indicate that brochs were fortified dwellings rather than the prehistoric equivalent of air-raid shelters.

The origin of brochs has also been much debated. One theory, that of John Hamilton, is that the broch developed in Orkney, perhaps from a blockhouse type of fortification, such as at Clickhimin (p. 60). A northern origin for brochs was also favoured by the excavators of Bu in Orkney. Here a structure with massively thick walls was described as a 'defended roundhouse', of proportions which could have developed into the solid-based northern broch.

Conversely, a western origin has been argued by Euan MacKie, who would see brochs developing from galleried duns and ultimately 'semi-brochs' such as Dun Ardtreck on Skye (p. 70). His theories rest largely on dates from his excavations of Dun Ardtreck and Dun Rhiroy in Ross and Cromarty.

The other major category of stone-built forts are the 'duns'. 'Dun' is an all-encompassing term which can include anything from small thick-walled homesteads to large sites closer to the size of hillforts. 'Dun' means 'a fortified place' and this is why many brochs have the 'dun' element in their names.

The distributions of brochs and duns are largely complementary. Most duns are in Argyll and adjacent regions including the Western Isles. Their numbers decrease towards the North where the concentration of brochs is greatest.

Brochs and duns are both regarded as belonging to the period around the first century BC and first two centuries AD, but the structures were often reused over many centuries. Like so many other 'Iron Age' sites, their chronology is also being extended backwards. Recent excavations at the dun of Balloch Hill, Argyll suggested that occupation spanned the sixth to the first centuries BC, and there is no reason why future excavations should not produce similar dates.

Although hillforts, brochs and duns were all defensive, the defences used varied greatly. In many instances, natural defences were made use of in addition to building man-made defences. Choosing a precipitous location greatly reduced the length of ramparts and walls which had to be built, as at Burgi Geos (p. 73) where only one short wall was needed to complete the defences.

Hillforts required greater lengths of man-made defences – often whole summits were surrounded by ramparts. This suggests that there was considerable manpower available for the construction, maintenance

Above *Dun Dornadilla, broch, with the Strathmore River in the background*

Below *Ardifuar dun, near Kilmartin, Mid Argyll. Many of the surrounding stone walls would probably have been built from the dun 'tumble'*

and defence of the long stretches of rampart. Brochs, however, could have been held effectively with only a few men. Broch defenders had the advantage of height, and could pitch weapons or boulders at anyone trying to scale or break through the walls. Similarly, promontory forts only had one wall or rampart which needed manning, and many sites could have been adequately defended by only a few people.

The communities occupying these various fortifications were very different. Many hillforts enclosed whole villages, and were probably also used for the coralling of livestock. Duns and promontory forts in contrast often had little room for more than two or three huts or lean-to structures.

Entrances to defended sites were often complex, involving tight turns between ramparts, which lessened the chances of head-on assault on the main gates. Broch entrances were built wide enough to admit only one person at a time, preventing mass attack on the doorway. Some brochs have chambers with floor slots directly above the entrance passage, so that anyone breaking through the door was open to attack from above.

Another device sometimes used was the *chevaux de frise*, rows of upright wooden or stone pillars set up in the area outside an entrance. These settings broke up and slowed down an attack either by foot or on horseback.

The importance of defence in the Bronze Age and Iron Age is seen not only in the number of defensive sites, but also in the range of weapons produced. Bronze Age weapons included spears, dirks and rapiers.

By the late Bronze Age, shields of leather and wood were being made, probably as a response to the use of bronze swords. Bronze shields, some decorated, have been found, but these may have been prestigious rather than practical.

Many of these weapons have been found in hoards. In Duddingston Loch, Edinburgh, for example, a large hoard was found in 1778 during dredging. Swords and spearheads were among the objects recovered. Some hoards may have been ritual, but the majority are believed to have been those of either traders or founders.

*Caisteal Grugaig broch, Lochalsh, looking at the entrance from the interior. Above the entrance is a recess or cell, presumably for observing those entering the broch*

There are several possible reasons for the increased need for defence in the Bronze and Iron Age periods in Scotland. Local feuds could have arisen over territory, seaways or grazing areas. In the 'heroic tales' of Ireland, which may reflect life in the early Iron Age, wealth was measured by the number of cattle which a group possessed, and obtaining cattle was the cause of countless raids.

A wider cause of many of the late troubles would have been the expansion of Roman control and consolidation of the Forth–Clyde frontier line. It is generally believed there was little resistance from the Lowland tribes. There are no records of battles, but some groups may have been dispossessed of their forts and lands. Population pressure may have been created in the North due to immigrants moving from the South and looking for new land.

Another possibility is that the stone forts of the North and West were built in response to the Roman slave trade. It has even been suggested that head-hunting was a common activity of Celtic tribes in Orkney and that this was the catalyst for fort-building.

None of these theories can be proven with certainty. What is certain from the scale of the fort-building is that the threats were not temporary, nor localised, and that troubled times continued for several centuries.

*Green Castle fort, East Lothian, its earthworks now marked by a grove of trees*

# DUN TELVE

Dun Telve and Dun Troddan (p. 54) more usually known as the Glenelg Brochs, are located in the valley of Glen Beag, Lochalsh. Dun Telve does not occupy a strong defensive position. Instead, it was built on the valley floor, near the river and presumably the best farmland.

A large part of the wall of Dun Telve is missing, and has been since the eighteenth century. Thomas Pennant

Right *The exterior of Dun Telve, just outside the entrance passage, showing the remains of a surrounding wall which may be of a later period than the broch*

Below *The interior of Dun Telve, showing the two scarcements, and voids*

*Looking from the interior of Dun Telve through the entrance passage, showing the doorway to a guard cell on the left, the door checks, lintel stone, and a cell above the passage*

*The courtyard of Dun Troddan showing the double galleried wall, the voids, entrance to the guard cell, scarcement and stairway entrance*

visited Dun Telve in 1772 during his 'Voyage to the Hebrides', and wrote:

> The more entire side appears of a most elegant taper form; the present height is thirty feet six inches; but in 1772 some Goth purloined from the top seven feet and a half [2.3m], under pretence of applying the material to certain public buildings.

Despite the missing portion, many of the 'classic' broch features are still visible, including the tapering or batter of the outer wall; scarcements or ledges, presumably for supporting an upper floor and the roof; the entrance with its bar-hole and door-checks; and the voids above the interior doors, probably designed to reduce weight on the lintels.

Around the broch are the remains of a number of outbuildings, including an oblong enclosure adjacent to the broch which the excavator, Alexander Curle, suggested was for the penning of livestock, but which may be later.

Among the artefacts recovered were three stone cups, carved from micaceous schist. Similar cups have been found at other brochs, and were perhaps oil lamps used to light the galleries and lower floors.

Some fragments of globular cooking vessels were also recovered, along with stone whorls and discs, some pieces of iron slag, a bronze ring and some quernstones, representing a wide range of activities.

# DUN TRODDAN

Dun Troddan (the Upper Broch) lies as its name suggests, higher up the glen than its neighbours Dun Telve (the Lower Broch). The greater part of the broch is only a few courses high, but for about a third of its diameter it rises to 7.5m (25ft).

The structure of the galleried wall can be seen in the broken section of the broch. In order to build a high wall in drystone, it is necessary to build wide foundations, but a solid, high, broad drystone wall would be very unstable due to its own weight. Building two parallel walls (each narrower than if it was standing alone) about one metre apart, is one way to tackle this problem. The walls are bonded together using horizontal stone slabs which, as well as holding the walls together, also form the gallery floors.

When the central area, or courtyard, was excavated by Alexander Curle, a number of interesting features were uncovered. In the primary levels, the remains of two stone-built hearths were found, and also eleven postholes, the remains of decayed wood still surviving in one of them.

The postholes were located in a circle 1.8–2m (6ft–7ft) out from the wall. It seemed logical to Curle that the holes originally contained posts supporting the front of a roof, the back of which rested on a scarcement. This arrangement may indicate a verandah-type of structure around the court, with the centre open to allow smoke to get out and light to get in. However, the amount of light getting into the broch in this way would have been negligible, and it is more likely the broch was completely roofed, as was the Hebridean Black House which had no provision for light or smoke.

A quantity of egg-shaped pebbles were found in the primary levels. The pebbles seemed to have been specially selected, but none showed signs of use. It is possible that they were collected for use as missiles.

*Right Dun Troddan broch, looking up the winding staircase, from ground level*

*The massive, blank wall of the exterior of Dun Troddan. An entrance round the other side would have been the only break in the walling*

# MOUSA

Situated on low ground near a pebbly shore, on the island of Mousa in Shetland, is the most complete of Scotland's brochs. It still survives to a height of just over 13m (43ft) but there may have been an additional metre to the wallhead. From a diameter of 15m (50ft) at the base, the broch tapers to 12m (40ft) in diameter at the top.

The walls are much thicker at the bottom. Typical of northern brochs, Mousa has a solid base, with the galleries beginning at a height of about 3m (10ft) above the ground. There are no guard cells off the entrance

*The Broch of Mousa with its classic 'cooling tower' outline, overlooking the southern entrance to Mousa Sound*

passage, but around the courtyard are entrances to three large cells within the base of the wall.

Two scarcement ledges run round the broch interior, one about 1.5m (5ft) above the floor level, the other a further 1.5m (5ft) higher. They would have held the beams of upper timber floors. It was from an upper floor, probably reached by a ladder, that access to the gallery was obtained. A stairway wound upwards between the galleried walls. The steps were narrow, rough and uneven allowing only toe or ball of foot purchase.

The survival of Mousa's walls to such a height is probably due to the fact that there was little secondary occupation of the broch, certainly no surrounding village on the scale of some other brochs like Gurness

*The remains of the wheelhouse built into the courtyard of the Broch of Mousa. The entrances lead to cells in the base of the broch*

# CARN LIATH

Carn Liath (the grey cairn) occupies a rocky terrace overlooking the Sutherland coast. It was first excavated in the nineteenth century by the Duke of Sutherland. Although the site first looked like a cairn, the remains of a broch were uncovered as the loose lichen-covered stones were cleared.

Pottery, flint chips, stone hammers, mortars and pestles, querns, whorls, shale rings, long-handled bone combs, a whale bone club, a silver fibula, steatite cups and an iron blade were among the artefacts recovered. These artefacts suggest that the site was inhabited over many centuries. Unfortunately, the site was not recorded accurately enough to allow its phases of occupation to be related to the artefacts.

Further excavations took place at the site in 1986. A chronology stretching as far back as the Bronze Age was established. A Bronze Age cist burial with a food vessel was discovered, and postholes indicated that a settlement existed on the site before the broch was built.

'Post-broch' settlement took the form of outbuildings in the area between the broch and the wall which surrounds the knoll on which the broch was built. Some of these buildings may have been contemporary with the use of the broch. A covered passage once led from the outer wall to the broch entrance.

(p. 69). There has been a great deal of controversy as to whether all brochs were 'broch towers' on the scale of Mousa. It is possible that many brochs did not reach such grand heights, but the amount of rubble found in and around others suggests that more than Mousa were true towers.

The structures in Mousa's courtyard are secondary to the broch's main period of use, and are the remains of a wheelhouse constructed in the third or fourth century AD.

This was not the last time that the broch was occupied. In the *Orkneyinga Saga* it is recorded that in AD 1153 Earl Harald sailed to Shetland from Caithness, on a mission to kill Erlend the Young who wanted to marry Harald's mother Margaret. The request had been refused by Harald, so Erlend had abducted Margaret from Orkney, sailed to Shetland 'and settled in the Broch on Mousa where everything had been made ready'.

Earl Harald arrived in Shetland and besieged the broch. This apparently was his only option, as the broch was considered too difficult to attack. Harald and Erlend eventually decided to negotiate. Erlend was given consent to marry Margaret, and in return Erlend supported Harald in his attempts to gain control of his Earldom.

Across Mousa Sound, on Shetland Mainland opposite Mousa, is another broch, the broch of Burraland. Mousa and Burraland were probably lookouts across the southern entry to the Sound, strategically positioned for observation of and quick action against any intruders.

*Carn Liath, looking through the entrance from the interior. In the background is the paved passage leading to the entrance through the outer wall*

# DUN NA MAIGH

Dun na Maigh broch is perched on the end of a spine of rock with extensive views over Tongue Bay and the surrounding hills of Sutherland.

Much of the broch has now collapsed – there is a pile of slipped masonry at the base of the crags, and the interior is also full of tumbled walling. The collapse was due largely to the broch being built right on the edge of the rock to make maximum use of the natural defences. The site was further fortified by a rampart which was built across the only side of the outcrop not defended by steep crags.

The broch entrance has survived despite the collapse. Instead of having only one set of door-checks along its passage, it has two sets, with a guard cell between. If stone slabs were used as doors, a great deal of protection would have been given against attack, even with fire. The low and narrow entrance passage would have made an attack on the doors, even with a battering ram, very difficult.

Below *The spine of rock which probably provided the builders of Dun na Maigh with the material for the broch. In the background is the Kyle of Tongue*

Right *Looking south across the interior of the broch of Dun na Maigh towards Ben Loyal*

# CLICKHIMIN

The environs of the settlement of Clickhimin in Shetland have changed dramatically since the site was inhabited. A housing estate now overlooks the site, with Lerwick camp site and the Clickhimin leisure centre on the adjacent shore. In addition, the water-level of the surrounding fresh water loch was lowered in the late nineteenth century, leaving the settlement on a promontory rather than on an islet joined to the shore by a causeway as it was previously.

The site was excavated by J.R.C. Hamilton in the

*Clickhimin settlement, looking northwards to the landing stage, the quay of upright stones, the fort, blockhouse and broch. The footmarked stone forms the threshold of the small gateway on the causeway*

1950s, and a complex settlement sequence was uncovered. The first occupation of the site was from around 700 BC. An oval stone-built house with alcoves around a central hearth was the main building. The inhabitants used barrel-shaped pottery vessels, and stone tools such as pounders and rubbers.

Some centuries later a massive enclosing wall was built around the island with the entrance through a free-standing blockhouse similar to that at Ness of Burgi (p. 72). The blockhouse was a galleried structure with bar-holes, guard cells, and a set of stone stairs, all features found in later brochs. Hamilton suggested that these architectural elements showed that the Shetland architects had mastered all the techniques necessary to build a 'true' broch, and he used the results of his

*Looking from the fort wall at Clickhimin towards the blockhouse, broch and entrance through the outer wall*

excavations at Clickhimin to propose that brochs developed in the North.

Timber lean-to structures were built around the interior of the fort. These may have been double storeyed with the upper floors used for habitation, and the ground level for cattle stalls and workshop space.

The broch at Clickhimin was probably built shortly after the blockhouse. It is one of few brochs to have two entrances, and has another interesting feature – the provision of a cell above the entrance passage with viewing slots to the entrance below. It would have been possible to spear intruders from above should the door have been breached.

Stone pounders, potlids, and beads were recovered from the broch levels, as well as oil lamps made from steatite and sandstone. Bone tools included awls, pins and a chisel, and there were bronze pins and iron tools, and a lot of pottery.

When the broch went out of use, a wheelhouse was inserted into its courtyard. Other huts were built between the broch and the enclosure wall, although their exact relationship to the broch and wheelhouse is not known.

Set into the path at the end of the causeway, there is a stone with two footprints pecked into its surface. These are believed to be linked with inaugural rites in Dark Age times. The stone is unlikely to be in its original setting.

# DUN TORCUILL

In Loch an Duin, a tidal loch near Lochmaddy, North Uist, is an island connected to the shore by a causeway. On the island, which may be partly man-made, are the remains of a ruined broch, Dun Torcuill.

The causeway is about 2m (6ft 6in) wide at its narrowest parts, and curves to make use of a rock sticking out of the loch half way between the shore and the islet. High tides sometimes flood the causeway.

The broch itself was built of good drystone walling.

*Dun Torcuill broch, situated in Loch an Duin, looking from the north at the causeway which connects it with the shore*

Details of the entrance, cells and gallery can be made out in the thickness of the wall, but the whole of the interior, almost to the height of the wall, is full of rubble and nettles.

On the west side of the islet are the outlines of some smaller structures. The fact that they seem to have been built from stones from the broch, that their masonry is different to that of the broch, and that one of the structures blocks the broch entrance, indicates that they are more recent structures, perhaps sheep pens.

The only other site in North Uist classified as a broch is Dun Sticer, which is in the same region as Dun Torcuill, and also built on an island with a connecting causeway.

# DUN CARLOWAY

One of Scotland's best preserved brochs is Dun Carloway on the island of Lewis. It exhibits most of the usual broch features, including two side cells leading off the courtyard.

In 1971 one of the cells was excavated. A series of deposits was uncovered, interpreted as a succession of hearths, probably later than the main period of use of the broch. From the lack of metalworking slag or domestic refuse, and the abundance of vessel sherds, the cell was thought to have been used for the firing of pottery.

*The interior of Dun Carloway, showing the scarcement, galleried wall, cell entrance on the right, and stair entrance on the left, with lintelled voids above*

*Dun Carloway broch, looking west at the batter of the wall, and showing the nature of the outcrop*

# DUN BEAG

One of the best preserved of Skye's brochs is Dun Beag which occupies a rocky knoll on a hillside overlooking Loch Bracadale, with extensive views to the Cuillin Hills and MacLeod's Tables. It was excavated between 1914 and 1920 by Countess Vincent Baillet de Latour. The central area, two cells, the staircase and a stretch of gallery were cleared during the excavations. Workmen sifted the 200 tons of stone and earth through their fingers.

For about half its circumference the broch is built very near to the edge of the knoll, which would have made the broch walls appear even taller and more impressive.

The entrance passage is paved, with the usual checks and bar-holes which probably held a slab door. Three entrances lead off the courtyard – one to a round corbelled cell, the second (now blocked) to a long stretch of gallery at ground level, and the third to a staircase which would have provided access to an upper gallery.

Artefacts found during the Countess's excavations were mainly domestic objects, including stone whorls, a steatite cup (possibly used as a lamp), stone scrapers, various pottery sherds from flat-based globular vessels and also personal objects such as glass beads and bronze wire rings and pins.

*Dun Beag broch, perched on its rocky eminence overlooking Loch Bracadale and Ardtreck peninsula*

*Part of the stairway in the gallery of the broch with some
fallen lintels in the foreground*

Many cattle and sheep bones were found during the excavations, mostly among the debris in the gallery, and probably from secondary occupation. Some carbonised seeds, however, were found in the early levels, and identified as either oats or rye.

Johnson and Boswell visited Dun Beag in 1773, and were greatly impressed, especially by the size of the lintels, some of which were still in position at that time. Johnson's somewhat patronising comment was that

> They were probably raised by putting long pieces of wood under them, to which the action of a long line of lifters might be applied. Savages, in all countries, have patience proportionate to their unskillfulness, and are content to attain their ends by very tedious methods.

In the north, folk tradition links the brochs to fairies, ghosts and spirits. It was thought to be dangerous to approach the brochs, especially after nightfall, when a strange green light was often seen emanating from them. Both humans and cattle captured by the fairies (*Sìthichean*) were taken to the brochs (*Sìthein*), which were thought to be entrances to the fairies' country. The brochs were said to be 'as old as the Sithichean', meaning older than man.

# CLACHTOLL

The broch near Clachtoll in Sutherland is built on a large expanse of rugged, jagged rocks, directly on the shore. It was once a massive and heavily defended broch with a strong outwork of walling which crossed the promontory. Between the broch and the wall are the outlines of stone huts.

The lintel on the exterior of the entrance passage is triangular. As well as being decorative, this shape of lintel would disperse the weight of the wall above more effectively than a straight lintel.

Right *Clachtoll broch, looking south-west over the large stones of the outwork towards the entrance with its massive triangular lintel still in position*

Below *The jagged and slanting outcrops below Clachtoll broch. It would have been relatively easy to split blocks from the bedrock*

# EDINSHALL

The broch of Edinshall in Berwick is one of very few brochs to be found outside the main concentration in the North and West. Various suggestions have been put forward to explain these 'outliers', one being that the professional broch-builders were commissioned by southern families to build the towers as protection against the Roman army.

The earliest structure at Edinshall was a fort, an oval area enclosed by a double rampart and ditches. It was built on a hillside above the Whiteadder Water. The broch itself was built in a corner of the fort. It is much larger than a typical northern broch, with an internal diameter of 17m (55ft). The walls are 5m (16ft) thick in places, and there are various cells within. Like most brochs, there are door checks and guard cells in the entrance passage. The general opinion is that, given its large diameter, it was never a high tower.

Within the ramparts are the outlines of various hut circles and enclosures, some built over the defences and obviously of a later date than the fort.

The broch and hut circles were excavated at various times during the nineteenth century, but these excavations helped little in understanding the site.

*Edinshall broch, fort and settlement, looking over the ramparts of the fort to the broch. The Whiteadder River runs along the valley below the site*

# MIDHOWE

Midhowe broch on Rousay, Orkney was built in a prominent position overlooking Eynhallow Sound. The land which it occupies has water on three sides – the shore at one side, and a geo on two others. A thick stone wall with a ditch on either side of it cuts the area off from the adjoining mainland. As the site is right on the shore, there has been substantial erosion resulting in the loss of some of the surrounding buildings, and a flagstone wall was built in the 1930s to protect it from further erosion. The landowner Walter Grant, who excavated the site between 1930 and 1933, later gave the monument to the State.

Originally the site seems to have consisted of only the broch and the rampart and ditches. It was not until later that the surrounding houses were built over the filled up inner ditch.

Unlike most of the northern brochs, Midhowe has a gallery within the wall at ground level. The gallery was apparently faulty in its design or building and at some point had to be filled in. Vertical slabs were leaned up against the external wall, providing a buttress to prevent the collapse of the outer wall.

The entrance to the broch has two sets of door-checks. There were two cells between the doors, one opening into a stretch of gallery. Inside the broch there were stairs at a higher level, indicating another gallery. A scarcement held the upper floor, apparently reached

*Midhowe broch, looking south across the later houses to the broch. Midhowe chambered cairn is in the building to the rear*

by a ladder. A stone stair leading up from the courtyard is a secondary construction.

Today the courtyard is divided in two by a partition of stone slabs, the remains of later habitation. Each half had a water tank and hearth, and was further partitioned. One hearth had a posthole on each side which would have supported a spit. The broch interior was

*The stone furnishings and secondary partitions of later occupation inside the broch courtyard. There is a hearth and tank on the left, and a tank set into the floor to the right of the partition*

*Looking south-east at the entrance of the broch at Midhowe, showing some of the external structures and the slab buttressing built to support the collapsing wall*

probably occupied by two families in its later phases of use.

Around the broch, only one building has survived completely. It was 'customised' to fit between the broch wall and the defensive wall and consists of various irregularly shaped rooms. Some of the surrounding buildings were used as workshops rather than dwellings. In one building an iron-smelting hearth was found, and there were also crucibles and moulds which had been used in the manufacture of bronze objects.

# GURNESS

The broch at Gurness was 'discovered' by the Orkney poet Robert Rendall. One day in the summer of 1929 he was sitting on the Knowe of Gurness sketching the view of Rousay Sound, when one of the legs of his stool slipped into the ground. On removing some of the stones he uncovered a descending set of stairs.

Excavations were carried out that year, and the broch along with an impressive arrangement of outbuildings, was recovered.

The broch is solid-based, and its dimensions suggest that it was once a considerable height, although at some point its upper sections had been dismantled, probably to provide the quantities of building stone

*Gurness broch, looking across the inner ditch from the middle rampart towards the broch with its surrounding, and probably later, buildings*

necessary for the surrounding buildings. As well as the usual features, the broch had a flight of steps leading down from the courtyard to an underground water tank filled from a spring.

Surrounding the broch were three sets of ditch and rampart. An entrance crossed these defences at the east.

The buildings around the broch were neatly constructed with flagstone walling. Upright slabs were used to partition the houses. Most of the buildings are circular huts, sometimes joined to form larger structures.

It is not certain that all these buildings were erected after the broch had gone out of use, but a bone knife handle with an ogam incised on it, and a stone with Pictish symbols carved on it, indicates a later date for at least some of them.

In addition to the round huts, a rectangular house was discovered. Rectangular building is usually attributed to Norse habitation. Although the artefacts associated with the house could not be specifically assigned to the Norse, the burial of a woman, dug into the rampart, gives evidence of Norse habitation of the site around the ninth century AD. The body had been laid in a stone-lined grave along with some possessions – a shell necklace, an iron sickle, a knife with a wooden handle, and two oval bronze brooches with intricate decoration. Fabric adhering to the back of one brooch showed that the body had been buried in a garment of finely woven wool.

# DUN ARDTRECK

Dun Ardtreck on Skye is a D-shaped galleried structure built on the edge of a promontory. Euan MacKie, who excavated part of the site in the 1960s, believed it demonstrated that brochs developed in the north-west of Scotland, from galleried duns. He used the term 'semi-broch' to describe Dun Ardtreck – a galleried dun with many of the features common to fully developed brochs.

The dun was built on a rubble platform, probably sometime in the first century BC. It consisted of a semi-circle of galleried walling with a sheer cliff forming the straight side of the D. A parapet may have edged the cliff. The entrance had bar-holes and door-checks, with a guard cell to one side, and opened into a courtyard with two further entrances leading to the galleries.

Early occupation seemed, from excavation evidence, to have been sporadic, and to have ended with the burning and destruction of the dun. Later the unstable parts of the dun walls were dismantled and the site began its life as a dwelling. A short flight of steps led up to the partially rubble-filled interior.

The most interesting find from the excavation was the doorhandle of the dun, a ring made from twisted strands of iron wires. It had been fused to some stones on the passage floor during the fire.

*Dun Ardtreck, looking towards the entrance. An outer wall surrounded the promontory*

# DUN GRUGAIG

Dun Grugaig, 'the wretched woman's dun', occupies a small promontory jutting into the sea along the coast of Sleat in the south of Skye. It is one of several duns which were sited at the coastal ends of small valleys of fertile land along this stretch of coastline.

At Dun Grugaig the promontory is very steep on all sides, and could only have been approached from the landward side where a thick, and presumably high, galleried wall crossed the promontory. Around the rest of the promontory are the faint traces of a much lower wall or parapet.

One of the dun's most impressive features is the lintel above the doorway, a massive triangular block. Several flat lintels remain in place across the entrance passage and the bar-holes and door-checks are still in place.

Inside the dun, a stairway led to a gallery in the wall above the entrance passage.

There are no traces of houses within the dun, but a metre above the present ground level is a scarcement which may have supported the roof timbers of some kind of 'lean-to' structure behind the main wall.

One suggestion for small promontory duns of this type is that they were lookout posts and signalling stations to warn neighbouring communities of approaching danger.

*Dun Grugaig, looking down from the higher adjoining mainland. A galleried wall crossed the promontory, and there would have been a lower parapet around the cliff edge*

# NESS OF BURGI

At the south end of Shetland Mainland, is a small headland with precipitous cliffs on its east and south. The headland is part of a larger promontory about ten acres in area, which is only accessible from the adjoining land over a narrow, natural rock arch.

Situated across the tip of the headland is the most obvious structure on the peninsula, a 'burgi' or 'blockhouse' similar to the one at Clickhimin (p. 60). It is a rectangular building with a passage running through it, opening into a 'courtyard' of level ground edged by cliffs. The passage would have been blocked by a barred door, the bar holes extending into two cells, one on each side of the passage. There was a third cell, now much damaged by erosion, probably entered from the end of the blockhouse.

In front of the blockhouse is a huge stone-built rampart, with a ditch cut into the rock on either side of it.

The site was partially excavated in the 1930s by Miss Cecil Mowbray, who examined the blockhouse. Bones of various animals, limpet shells and pottery fragments were found. Unfortunately there was no excavation of the courtyard to establish the existence of huts or shelters. Erosion has made the courtyard appear smaller than it would have been originally.

*Ness of Burgi fort, looking over the headland to the outer defences with the blockhouse to the rear. The outer rampart shows in section above the chasm*

# BURGI GEOS

Occupying a precipitous promontory on the west coast of Yell in Shetland is the fort of Burgi Geos. The setting is spectacular, with cliffs rising starkly from the sea below.

Burgi Geos is often referred to as the site of a broch, but the structure is more like a blockhouse. Today little remains of this once solid building. The approach to the peninsula where the blockhouse stands is along a neck of land 37m (120ft) long and only 3–6m (10-20ft) wide. Along each side of the path are upright stone slabs, presumably to minimise the risk of falling onto the jagged cliffs below.

It is not just the promontory which was defended. The larger adjoining headland also had a wall crossing its neck, and around the cliff edge are signs of a parapet. Although nothing is known of the archaeology of the interior of the headland, one possibility is that it was occupied by dwellings with the promontory being used as a signalling station or lookout post. It is difficult to believe that the promontory itself would have been continually occupied.

*The precipitous promontory of Burgi Geos. The blockhouse wall can be seen crossing the promontory, while lining the narrow approach are a row of flat slabs*

# DUN GERASHADER

Dun Gerashader on Skye is a large dun which has been built on the summit of a high rocky eminence. There is only one direction of easy approach to the plateau and this has been cut off by a massive rampart 4m (13ft) thick.

The rampart's defences have been further strengthened by the placing of lines of boulders across the slopes of the eminence, in the style of a *chevaux de frise*. Any attack on the rampart either on foot or by horseback would have been impeded by these obstacles.

Above *The lines of boulder defences on the slope leading up to the rampart of Dun Gerashader, Skye*

Below *Looking over two lines of boulder defences to the massive rampart which cuts off the end of the promontory. 'The Old Man of Storr' is the rock formation in the background*

# DUN GRUGAIG

Further up Glen Beag than the Dun Telve and Dun Troddan brochs (p. 52), is a galleried dun, Dun Grugaig, which has been built on a rocky knoll on the hillside.

The dun is D-shaped, and although tumbled in places, chambers within the wall, a scarcement and an entrance passage with door checks can be made out among the debris.

An unusual feature of the site is the way in which a crevice in the knoll was filled with walling to allow building to continue across it.

*Dun Grugaig, Glen Beag, showing its situation on a rocky outcrop. A river flows directly behind the knoll at the bottom of a deep gorge*

*A detail of the walling on the north side of Dun Grugaig, showing the way in which a crevice had been filled*

# CASTLE HAVEN

The only known galleried dun in Galloway is Castle Haven. Its impressive height is due largely to extensive restoration by James Brown, laird of Knockbrex, in 1905.

The dun is D-shaped, with a central courtyard. Leading off the courtyard are six entrances to the gallery within the wall. Instead of a staircase, stone slabs projected from the wall in a stile arrangement.

Artefacts found during the restoration included quernstone fragments, whetstones, a polished stone disc, and a fragment of an amber bead.

Below *The interior of Castle Haven, showing its D-shaped plan and part of the galleried wall with the entrances to it leading off the courtyard*

Above *The stile-type steps leading up the inner wall of Castle Haven beside the entrance to a cell within the wall*

# KEMP'S WALK

The fort at Larbrax, 'Kemp's Walk' is the largest of western Galloway's promontory forts. The promontory overlooks Broadsea Bay. On its south and west sides, grassy banks slope very steeply for 60–70m (200–230ft) down to the shore, while on the east side the land drops down to a small burn in a deep glen.

The fort occupies the end of the promontory. Heavy man-made defences cross the promontory on its north side, the only direction from which access is easy. Three ramparts formed of soil and gravel, with ditches between, cut across the neck of the promontory. It is possible that there was a smaller rampart around the edge of the promontory but if this was the case, no trace now remains.

An area measuring about 83 by 44m (270 by 145ft) is enclosed by the ramparts and the steep sides of the head of the promontory. There are no signs of hut circles within the enclosed area, but on a narrow spur of land, jutting out to the west, is a little hillock occupied by what seems to have been a hut circle.

*Kemp's Walk promontory fort, looking west. The outlines of the ramparts can be seen clearly, cutting off access to the end of the promontory*

# EILDON HILL

Eildon Hill North fort, which may derive its name from the Anglo Saxon 'Æled dun', the 'Fire Hill', occupies one of a line of hills overlooking the Tweed and the Leader Water. The hill could have taken its name from the Roman signal station on the summit. A rectangular wooden tower stood within a circular enclosure on the northern side of the hill. The ground floor was paved and the tower had a tiled roof. The hilltop could have been seen for over 30km (20 miles) in all directions except from the south-west.

Like so many of the large southern hillforts, Eildon Hill had several phases of occupation. The earliest structure on the hilltop was a single rampart enclosing about 3.6 hectares. In its final phase it had three concentric ramparts which may have been built on specially prepared terraces.

The summit is pitted with hut platforms, about 300 in all. If these were occupied simultaneously, this could suggest a population of between 1000–2000 people. A village of this size would indicate that the occupants traded with other groups in the area to obtain some of the food they needed, perhaps in exchange for manufactured items. It is believed that this site was the capital of the Selgovae tribe, known to live in the area of the Upper Tweed.

*Eildon Hill North fort, later used as a Roman signal station, occupied the hill on the right of the photo*

# BROWN CATERTHUN AND WHITE CATERTHUN

The forts of Brown Caterthun and White Caterthun occupy the summits of two hills in Angus, just over 2.5km (1½ miles) apart. The 'Brown' and 'White' in the name refers to the appearance of the ramparts. Those on the summit of White Caterthun comprise a mass of grey boulders, while the ramparts of Brown Caterthun are all heather-covered.

The defences of the Brown Caterthun are made up of several lines of rampart encircling the hilltop. The innermost enclosure is a ruined stone wall, the area within measuring 90 by 60m (300 × 200ft). Further down the hill is a thick wall surrounded by double ramparts with a ditch between them. This wall has nine entrances through it, some of which match with entrances in the ramparts. Still further down the slopes are two more ramparts with an external ditch enclosing an area 330m by 310m (1100 by 1020 ft).

White Caterthun fort occupies a slightly higher hill, the summit of which is enclosed by a pair of concentric walls. These are now ruined, and the combined boulder mass is spread over about 30m (100ft). Originally the inner wall was about 12m (40ft) thick, the outer one 6m thick, and the area enclosed was 140 by 60m (460 by 200ft), smaller than its neighbour.

There is unfortunately no dating evidence for the hillforts, so it is uncertain if they were contemporary to each other. Nor do we know how many occupational phases the ramparts represent.

*Looking over the inner stone ramparts of White Caterthun towards the hilltop occupied by the defences of Brown Caterthun*

# TYNRON DOON

The fort of Tynron Doon is a prominent feature in the hilly farmland of Nithsdale, in the south-west of Scotland. The profile of its ramparts can be clearly seen, sculptured from the hilltop. The rocky peak is a spur of Auchengibbert Hill, and was obviously chosen for its strong natural defences, and commanding views.

The summit itself is surrounded by a drystone wall, and there is a further stretch of walling along a terrace on the north east. On the more gently sloping west and south-west aspects, three steep-sided ramparts have been built one in front of the other, separated by deep ditches which presumably provided the earth and stone for the ramparts.

There are various structural remains, mainly the circular platforms of huts, within the enclosure. A hut circle 4.6m (15ft) in diameter lies just inside the entrance. Apparently the fort was again occupied much later. An L-shaped tower house, probably belonging to the late sixteenth century, was built in the north-west corner of the enclosure. Finds from the fort and the slopes reflect the long use of the site from the Iron Age on.

*Tynron Doon fort, looking north-east. The profile of the ramparts can be made out, defending the fort along its more vulnerable western slopes*

# ARBORY HILL

The summit of Arbory Hill in Clydesdale is ringed by three distinct lines of defences, representing two phases of fort building.

The earlier fort enclosed an area 82 by 69m (270 by 226ft) and consisted of two ramparts constructed largely from material dug from two external ditches. The defences were cut by five entrances, an unusually high number. The ramparts are concentric apart from a stretch where the distance between them widens and the space could have been used for the corralling and protection of cattle and sheep.

*Arbory Hill fort looking north-west, showing the linear earthwork running across the saddle of the hill, with the three lines of defences around the summit*

The later fort was built inside the inner rampart of the earlier structure. It was a circular enclosure with a stone wall about 3m (10ft) thick, broken by two entrances and enclosing an area half that of the former fort.

Inside this second enclosure are the outlines of three ring-ditch houses and a hut platform, and there are also traces of buildings between the inner rampart of the earlier fort and the wall of the later fort.

Seventy-five metres (245ft) from the fort, across the hillside, cutting off the higher ground to the east, is a further earthwork, possibly another line of defence. Alternatively it could have been a barrier to separate cattle from crops growing around the fort – cultivation traces have been identified beyond the outer rampart.

# CADEMUIR HILL

Overlooking the Tweed Valley, on the high Cademuir Hills are two hillforts, occupying the same ridge.

Cademuir I is the higher of the two, and comprises a 3m (10ft) thick stone wall which enclosed at least 35 timber huts.

The second fort is smaller with a 6m (20ft) thick wall and various other enclosures around it. A *chevaux de frise* was set up in such a way that it would have been hidden from attackers approaching from the north-east.

Right *Looking south towards a ridge of the Cademuir Hills, each summit occupied by a hillfort*

Below *Some of the 100 remaining stones of Cademuir II's* chevaux de frise *with the ramparts on the right*

# DREVA CRAIG

The fort on Dreva Craig in Tweeddale was strategically positioned to command the eastern end of the Biggar Gap, the valley which allows access between the upper stretches of the Rivers Tweed and Clyde.

Two stone ramparts surrounded the hilltop, the area enclosed by the inner one being 60 by 45m (200 by 150ft). Each rampart was over 4m (13ft) thick, faced with boulders with stone packing between. There are no signs of buildings within the enclosure, but it is possible that there were lean-to structures against the rampart. There are some later stone-built structures, one partially built into the tumble from the outer rampart.

Although Dreva Craig occupies a lofty position, its natural defences are not strong. In an attempt to overcome this a stone *chevaux de frise*, extending over a 650m$^2$ (770yd$^2$) area, was constructed on the south-west beyond the outer rampart. Over 100 of the stones remain in position, and there are many more which have fallen. A similar obstacle appears to have been constructed on the north-east slope.

Below the fort, on the northern side of the hill are the remains of an undefended settlement, with a field system running down the slope. It is not known if this settlement was contemporary with the fort.

*The ramparts of Dreva Craig, looking south-west at the* chevaux de frise *beyond the outer rampart*

# FINAVON

The fort of Finavon occupies the summit of the northernmost ridge of Finavon Hill, overlooking the south Esk in Angus. Unlike most hillforts, the ramparts do not follow the contours of the hill, but are almost straight, a desire to save on labour and material being suggested by the excavator V.G. Childe.

The ramparts were massive, over 6m (20ft) thick, the bottom sections being built of sandstone walling. Signs of vitrification (stones fused by intense heat) were found in the core of the wall, extending 2m (6ft) into the core, but the wall faces were unaltered.

Vitrification implies that the fort had a timber framework, burning timber providing the intensity of heat capable of vitrifying the stones. Vitrification probably came about when a site was under attack but it has also been suggested that burning was deliberate in some cases with the intentions of producing a more solid rampart.

Current research is focusing on the possibilities of dating vitrified material from forts by thermoluminescence, a technique used to pinpoint the date of pottery firing.

*Finavon vitrified fort, Forfar, Angus, looking up at the ramparts towards the north-east*

# TAP O'NOTH

Tap o'Noth hillfort sits atop a prominent hill of rounded profile rising from the fertile cultivated valleys and rolling countryside near Rhynie in Gordon. The hill is visible from 50km (30 miles) away.

The summit is surrounded by a single stone rampart which may originally have been 6–8m (20–26ft) thick and enclosed a rectangular area 105 by 40m (345 by 130ft). The rampart was timber-laced and vitrified in stretches.

Slightly further down the hill is another rampart, a stone wall with a boulder core. This defence may be earlier than the vitrified one. Within the enclosure are about 150 possible hut-circles. Many of them are on the northern slope of the hill, which was probably sheltered from the prevailing wind. Some may be quarry sites rather than hut circles.

The date of the fort is not certain, but three glass beads from near the lower wall suggest a late Iron Age date.

*The massive wall of the upper enclosure on Tap o'Noth, Gordon*

# DUNNIDEER

On the Hill of Dunnideer in Gordon sits a ruined medieval tower, one of the earliest in Scotland, having been built around 1260. The tower was constructed largely from vitrified material taken from an earlier hillfort in which it stands.

The vitrified fort comprised a single rampart enclosing a rectangular area with rounded corners, measuring 65 by 25m (210 by 80ft). The impressions of timbers which laced the stone rampart can be seen in the vitrified stonework in some stretches.

Lower down the hill are the outlines of two other ramparts, both unfinished. The external one is little more than a marker trench, but sections of the internal one showed the beginnings of rampart construction. It is not clear which was earlier – the unfinished hillfort or the vitrified fort.

It is an old tradition that sheep which graze on the Hill of Dunnideer have 'teeth of gold'. The teeth seem to be covered in a yellow coating with a metallic sheen assumed to be gold. It is thought that this is actually a deposit from the saliva, made up of lime, phosphoric oxide and organic matter, laid down in microscopic layers. The metallic appearance is due to the refraction of light by the overlapping layers.

*The summit of Dunnideer Hill, with part of the vitrified rampart in the foreground, and the ruin of the medieval castle beyond*

# WODEN LAW

Woden Law is the southern eminence of a spur of the Cheviot Hills. Views from the summit are extensive. The site was strategically important during Roman times, being close to the line of Dere Street, the route between York and the Firth of Forth.

The first structure on the summit was a native

*The view from the fort on Woden Law. Dere Street ran from the bottom right corner of the picture across the river and then northwards past the Pennymuir practice camps. The modern road marks its course until the crossroads by the forestry plantation where the road veers left and Dere Street continues straight on towards the far plantations*

hillfort. From excavations carried out on the ramparts it seems that the fort was constructed in several phases. First, an oval stone wall was built, and this was surrounded by two ramparts with a ditch between. At a later stage, after these ramparts had been destroyed by Roman activity on the site, the fort was again occupied by native groups, who built another enclosure on the summit.

The Romans constructed practice siegeworks consisting of two banks and three ditches. The outer bank has some flattened platforms, presumably for siege engines. Four camps at Pennymuir in the valley on the line of Dere Street are believed to have been a base for troops training in the area.

# NORTH BERWICK LAW AND THE CHESTERS

Separated by several miles of plain are the forts of North Berwick Law and the Chesters. They occupy very different locations. The Chesters is positioned on a low ridge, while the other fort has a much more dramatic location, on the summit of North Berwick Law, a conspicuous hill in the otherwise flat countryside of East Lothian.

The Chesters hillfort is oval with a complex series of ramparts, as well as various stretches of walling. The inner rampart, now largely ruined, encloses an area 119 by 49m (390 by 160ft). Surrounding this is a further rampart, which in turn is surrounded by the traces of up to six more.

The most unusual feature of the Chesters is its position, which seems to be extremely vulnerable. A rocky scarp towers 15m (50ft) above it, and from this position it would have been very easy to lob missiles into the interior of the fort.

Within the ramparts are traces of a large number of hut circles varying in diameter from 4.5–12m (15–40ft), the majority of which were built in the shelter of the inner wall.

The site has not been excavated, but it is probable that the ramparts were added to over a long period. Some of the hut circles overlap the inner, and probably earlier, ramparts. The site may represent a defended farming settlement, as the surrounding land is very fertile.

The natural defences of North Berwick Law are much more impressive. On all sides apart from the

*The Chesters Fort, looking west at the grass-covered defences of the eastern entrance*

south, the hillside rises steeply, almost vertically in parts. Little of the man-made defences now remain, but the hilltop seems to have been enclosed by a stone wall running 15m (50ft) below the summit. A second wall enclosed a lower terrace, and below this was a third enclosure on the gentler slopes, containing the remains of various hut circles.

Right *Looking over the ramparts of the Chesters fort towards North Berwick Law on the horizon*

# BURNSWARK HILL

The twin summits of Burnswark Hill in Annandale and Eskdale are surrounded by the ramparts of an Iron Age fort. For most of the circumference there is a single rampart, but on the south, where the slopes are gentler, is a double rampart.

Further down the hill, on both the northern and southern flanks, are the outlines of two rectangular Roman camps. The southern camp is the larger of the two, and has three artillery platforms, known locally as the 'Three Brethren', facing uphill towards the gateways of the hillfort, just over 120m (395ft) away.

When the site was first excavated in the late nineteenth century it was concluded that the Roman camps were built during a siege of the hillfort. Lead sling-bullets and balista balls were discovered in the southern camp. More were found nearer the summit, some with signs of impact, all adding weight to the siege theory.

Recent excavations, however, have shown that the defences on the summit were actually disused and tumbled when they came under fire from the Roman artillery. This suggests that an abandoned fort was being used by the Roman troops for target practice, although it is possible that this came about after a genuine confrontation with the occupants.

*Looking across the southern Roman camp on Burnswark Hill to the three artillery platforms on its upper limit, with the native hillfort in the background*

# FOUR
# TOMBS AND BURIAL

Artist's impression of Rudh' an Dunain chambered tomb in use. The entrance blocking has been removed to allow excarnated remains to be inserted. The ceremony is taking place at sunrise so that light will flood into the spirit-filled chamber.

The excavations uncovered bird bones, possibly signs of a 'bird cult', as with Isbister (Tomb of the Eagles). A bird is shown on the slab with the human bones, and the participants wear feathers in their hair, and feather cloaks.

Scotland is rich in impressive burial monuments, the enduring foci of countless ceremonies and rituals, spiritual touchstones shaped into the landscape. Excavation of these monuments can only hint at the beliefs, fears and superstitions of the communities which built them.

The oldest burial monuments in Scotland are the chambered tombs, built by Neolithic communities to house their dead. These tombs were for collective burials, and could be opened and closed as necessary, perhaps over a span of generations, until being sealed after the final burial.

*The Chambered Tombs of Scotland*, a detailed study of the monuments by Audrey Henshall, was published in 1963 and 1972. By studying the architectural features of the monuments, she divided the tombs into varying groups, the five main ones being:

– Bargrennan passage graves (found mainly in south-west Scotland)
– Clyde tombs (found mainly in Argyll and Arran)
– Orkney-Cromarty-Hebridean passage graves (from the north and north-west)
– Maes Howe passage graves (only found in Orkney), and
– Clava passage graves (with a mainly north-easterly distribution around Inverness).

Chambered tombs are found in many parts of Continental Europe. In Britain their distribution is mainly western, suggesting a movement via the Irish Sea. In addition to the above groups there are, in the southern parts of Scotland, some examples of earthern long barrows and long cairns, suggesting a spread of ideas, or people from the north-east of England.

All the tombs follow the same basic design principle – a burial chamber relatively small compared with the

*Corriechrevie cairn, Kintyre, looking west over a partly ploughed field*

size of the mound and entered along a low narrow passage. Regional variations may represent different rituals or building styles, but are probably governed largely by the available local stone. In Orkney, for example, where the bedrock is comprised mainly of sandstone flags, much use was made of slab partitioning and lintels. In other areas, more use had to be made of corbelling for roofing chambers and cells.

Burial evidence varies in quality from site to site. Treasure-hunting antiquarians have destroyed valuable information from some of the most obvious tombs, digging haphazardly into the central chambers and pilfering the contents. Looting goes back even further – there is evidence that Maes Howe (p. 96) was entered as early as Norse times.

Natural causes have also taken their toll at many sites. In areas with acid soils, bones will not survive, so information on the numbers of individuals buried, and their age and sex is lost. Fortunately, at some sites, such as Quanterness on Orkney mainland, the contents have

*The site of Auchagallon, on Arran, is sometimes described as a stone circle, but could equally be a cairn, or a combination of both. Only excavation will resolve this question*

survived well, providing some indication of the wealth of information which has been lost at other sites.

The main chamber and one of six side chambers was excavated in 1972–4 by Colin Renfrew. The human bones recovered represented 10 infants (up to 2 years old), 26 children (2–12 years), 36 teenagers (13–19 years) and 85 adults (20 years old or more). Of those teenagers and adults in which sex could be determined, 32 males and 27 females were identified. This indicates that for the population using the Quanterness tomb, and probably many other tombs, burial in the chambers was not closed on grounds of age or sex.

At sites where bones survive well, palaeopathologists can study burial remains for indications of diet, disease and fracture. Vitamin deficiences can be detected through skeletal deformities, and while many illnesses leave no permanent trace in the bones, degenerative disease of the spine stood out as a common condition at Quanterness, as well as at the nearby tomb of Isbister (p. 100).

Attempts are sometimes made to estimate the population of a community from the number of bones in a tomb. Such attempts are complicated by many unknown factors, such as how long a tomb was in use, and the unlikelihood that everyone in the community was buried in the tomb. At some sites the skeletons are incomplete, indicating that bones were removed. There is the added problem of knowing the size of the 'catchment area' for tombs: some groups may have travelled a long distance to bury their dead in a specific tomb.

Pottery sherds, stone tools, and bird and animal bones are often found in addition to the human bones. Rather than individual grave goods, some of these finds are probably the remains of feasting and rituals which were carried out at the time of a burial. Tombs may have been regarded as 'the houses of ancestors', the venues for feasting and offerings at many times of the year to call on the help of the ancestors in ensuring a good harvest or in ridding livestock of disease. Even where evidence from the tombs is well preserved, there are still many aspects of these rituals which can only be imagined – the members of the community taking part, the costumes and tattoos, the length and timing of ceremonies, the chanting and the dancing.

Chambered tombs were probably being erected in Scotland from the early fourth millennium BC onwards. The organization and time involved in transporting the materials and building the tombs would have been considerable. Quarrying and building work was probably done at a point in the farming year when manpower could be spared, perhaps between sowing and harvest.

The end product was more than purely utilitarian, as it would have been easier to bury the dead in simple graves dug into the ground. The size of the mounds and the effort involved suggests a certain communal pride – a statement of the power and wealth of a group. The finished tombs would have been objects of admiration by neighbouring tribes and visitors.

Burial in communal tombs was practised until around 2000 BC, by when the fashion had begun to move towards individual inhumation (burial). Communal burial, with its disarticulated stacks of bones, suggests the honouring and remembrance of 'ancestors' rather than the memory of any individual. The practice of

*The chambered cairn of Barpa Langass, North Uist, showing the large slabs which form the interior of the chamber*

single inhumation seems to herald a major social change in which certain individuals emerge in importance, either because of their social position or wealth. Both inhumations and cremations are known for the Bronze Age, often accompanied by personal grave goods such as jewellery, tools and weapons, which may reflect the status, occupation, or even the personality of an individual.

Beaker pottery often accompanied the early individual inhumations, and sometimes cremations, as did the larger 'food vessels'. These burials were often made in a cist, sometimes with a covering mound. Not all Bronze Age burials were accompanied by pottery. Burials under kerb-cairns (small cairns with a kerb of larger stones), for example, rarely included pottery.

Another burial practice introduced in the early part of the Bronze Age was the use of large urns to hold cremated remains. These urns are sometimes found in cemeteries as at Loanhead of Daviot (p. 170).

For the later prehistoric period there is little evidence for burial practice, although some ring cairns and cists are known. Outside the hillfort of Broxmouth near Dunbar, a cemetery of nine inhumations was uncovered beyond the fortifications. Most of the graves were stone-lined and covered with slabs. In addition, groups of barrows surrounded by square ditches, similar to some Iron Age burial sites in Yorkshire, have been identified in Angus by aerial survey. Cremated remains might also have been scattered, leaving no trace in the archaeological record.

# WIDEFORD HILL

Wideford Hill chambered cairn is situated on the western slope of the same valley as Cuween chambered cairn (p. 101). George Petrie excavated the tomb in 1849, and described it as a conical-shaped, turf-covered mound, 'contrasting pleasantly with the surrounding heather'. He noted that the mound was composed largely of clay.

The tomb is dug into the hillside, with the entrance facing downslope. The cairn has three drystone 'skins'; a central casing enclosing the chamber and passage, with two concentric vertical walls each over 1m (3ft 3in) thick around this. In Maes Howe fashion, three cells lead off the central area. The north cell has been cut into the bedrock.

The excavator found the roofed chamber to be intact but filled two thirds full of rubble which included horse, cow, deer, sheep and pig bones. The filling rose above the level of the passage, so it could not have been brought in via the entrance. The cells were empty. The most logical explanation is that the rubble was dropped in through a hole in the roof. Petrie had noticed a 'chimney-like' structure which he thought may have been built with this in mind.

*Wideford Hill chambered cairn, with its three-skin construction, showing how the tomb has been cut into the hillside*

# MAES HOWE

In 1861 James Farrer and his workmen began digging into the top of a large burial mound near Tormiston Mill on Orkney Mainland. On reaching the slabs covering the chamber roof, they found that they had been broken previously, and stones and earth had slipped into the chamber. The removal of the rubble took several days, and when at last it was possible to lower himself down the shaft and inspect the chamber, Farrer found that he was not, as suspected, the first to enter the tomb in that way.

Resting on the floor were three rectangular sand-

stone blocks which had been pulled from the openings to cells set into three of the walls. Engraved on the wall were a series of runes, and on a stone buttress were three carvings – a serpent, a walrus and a dragon. All that Farrer found was one fragment of human skull and some animal bones.

Thousands of people have visited the tomb of Maes Howe since Farrer. Situated near the Ring of Brodgar and the Stones of Stenness, it is one of the finest monuments of prehistoric Scotland. Its superb masonry and engineering are a testament to the skill of its Neolithic builders. Maes Howe gives its name to the classification of at least twelve similar tombs found only in Orkney.

The Maes Howe type of tomb has a narrow passage

*Maes Howe, looking along the passage towards the chamber from the entrance. The blocking stone is in the recess to the left*

*The northern corner of the chamber of Maes Howe,*
*detailing the buttressing with its tapering orthostat, the*
*corbelling of the roof, and the entrances to two of the side*
*cells*

leading to a central rectangular or square chamber, with side cells leading off it. At Maes Howe itself, the mound is built on a circular platform, flattened from an existing glacial hillock, and surrounded by a ditch and low bank. Clay and stones, now grass-covered, make up the body of the cairn, but around the chamber is a casing of stones. The hardening of the clay on construction has meant that the outline of the mound is almost certainly the same today as when it was built 5000 years ago.

The chamber at Maes Howe is 4.5m (15ft) square, and would originally have measured about 4.5m (15ft) from floor to capping stones. (A stone and concrete dome now forms the top of the roof.) The symmetry of the room is striking: the passage enters midway along one wall, and there is an opening to a side chamber midway along each of the other walls.

The corbelling of the walls begins only 1.4m (4ft 8in) above the floor and is supported by a buttress in each corner of the chamber. One face of each buttress is formed by a single tapering orthostat, an impressive contrast to the horizontal courses of the walls.

The smoothness of the building was due largely to the use of Orkney flagstone which splits neatly into thin slabs. The natural splitting was apparently not enough for the builders; the blocks were dressed further and the edges of the corbelled courses rounded off.

Some of the largest stones in the monument are the massive slabs of the entrance passage. The walls and most of the roof were each formed of a single slab. One of the wall slabs measures 5.6 by 1.3 by 0.18m (18 by 4ft

by 6in) and is estimated to weigh about 3 tons. The floor was paved with a further three large slabs, but when the tomb was opened this flooring was found to be covered with a layer of stones 0.5m (1ft 6in) deep. The accurate positioning of the slabs would have required careful manoeuvering with pulleys and rollers. It has been estimated that the building of Maes Howe, including the quarrying and transportation, could have taken almost 39,000 man-hours.

As the original contents of the tomb are unknown to us, it is very difficult to speculate on rituals carried out at the site. The fact that the entrance faces south-west suggests that the builders of Maes Howe had an interest in the winter sunset. Just inside the entrance is a triangular recess containing a huge stone which would have been pulled into the entrance to block the passage, perhaps between burials. This stone does not fit tightly – there is a gap of 0.5m (1ft 6in) between the top of the stone and the lintel when it is in the 'closed' position. From the accurate fit of the stones in the rest of the tomb, this must have been intentional. At mid-winter, light from the setting sun would have streamed through the gap and down the passage.

'It is long ago that a great treasure was hidden here' reads one of the runic inscriptions carved on the chamber walls. This, along with references in the *Orkneyinga Saga*, and the animal carvings, Scandinavian in style, suggests that the chamber was entered on more than one occasion in the twelfth century.

The *Orkneyinga Saga* related that at the time when Earls Erlend and Harald were fighting for control of the Earldom, Harald and some of his followers sheltered in the tomb during a snowstorm. The visit was said to have been such a terrible experience that certain members of the party went mad, slowing down the group's progress considerably.

Other runic inscriptions state that a group of crusaders met up at the tomb before going on to the Holy Land.

The results of recent excavations by Colin Renfrew indicate that the 'great treasure' alluded to by the Norse visitors may have been Viking rather than Neolithic. Rebuilding of the bank around the mound was radiocarbon dated to the ninth century AD, suggesting that reuse of the tomb, perhaps even for the burial of a Viking chieftain.

In local folklore, Maes Howe was believed to have been inhabited by a very strong goblin, the Hogboy, perhaps derived from Haugbuie, Norse for 'The Ghost of the Tomb'.

# QUOYNESS

Sanday, one of the more northerly of the Orkney islands, today has a population of about 600, mainly farming people. In the past, the island probably supported a much larger population. Sanday paid one sixth of all the tax of the Orkneys in Viking times, taxes being levied in proportion to the agricultural yield of the islands.

Although such statistics for prehistoric times are lacking, the number of Neolithic and Bronze Age burial grounds on the island also suggest a sizeable population. On the isolated peninsula of Els Ness is one of the Neolithic burial complexes, comprising two chambered tombs and numerous burial mounds. The most complete of the tombs is Quoyness. Nearby lies the tomb of Edmondshowe, which is itself enclosed by an arc of eleven Bronze Age burial mounds connected by an earthen bank. At least another 26 cairns are dotted over the peninsula, and one can only guess how many more have been flattened by the wind and rain.

Quoyness is built in a similar tradition to Maes Howe, having a main chamber with six side cells leading off it. The chamber walls were built of large water-worn stones. Slabs bonded into both faces at the corners gave the structure stability. The mound has an interesting construction, with three wall-faces, the inner one enclosing the chambers and cells. The middle wall-face retains the loose mound material, while the outer wall-face blocked the entrance, and was constructed during the final sealing of the tomb.

*General view of the exterior of Quoyness. Since consolidation, the two concentric wall faces can be seen, with the grass-covered rubble platform in the foreground*

The dome-shaped mound was built on a raised platform, surrounded by a neat kerb of stones about 0.5m (1ft 6in) high. Because none of the gentle low slopes of Sanday reach more than 15m (50ft) above sea level, the tomb would have stood out from its surroundings.

The cairn was excavated in 1867 by Farrer and Petrie, who expected the mound to contain a broch. Bones and skulls were found in four of the cells (the two opposite the main entrance contained no remains). Further skeletal fragments, representing at least ten adults and four children, were found in a stone-lined cist in the floor of the main chamber. In his excavation notes Petrie wrote: 'on lifting the cover of the corner cist, saw it to be full of bones, coloured very black – seemed pretty whole and observed apparently human thigh bones and leg bones but no trace of skulls.'

Apart from the cist, a shallow trench had been dug into the floor of the cell. There were no human bones in it, only loose 'rubbish'.

Objects from in and around the tomb included a polished slate 'hammerhead' and a polished bone pin, similar to objects found at the Neolithic village of Skara Brae. This, along with radiocarbon dating of human bones excavated by Childe in the 1950s, suggests that the tomb was in use in the early third millennium BC.

*Detail of Quoyness chamber, showing the oblique slabs bonding the walls at the corners. The walls are built directly onto the natural clay floor*

*Inside the chamber of Quoyness, looking south-west and
showing the entrances to three of the chambers. The stone
courses overlap slightly and converge towards the roof*

# ISBISTER

Isbister, more popularly known as 'the Tomb of the Eagles' (after the remains of white-tailed eagles found within), is perched above a sheer cliff on the island of South Ronaldsay in the Orkney Islands. The entrance faces out to the sea – a breathtaking aspect especially on a stormy day.

Isbister appears to be a stalled cairn at first sight, but actually has three side cells leading off the main chamber in a similar way to the Maes Howe sites. Four pairs of slabs project from the wall of the main chamber, but two of the pairs project only slightly, so the overall effect is of a large passage with a smaller area divided off at each end. These end sections have flagged floors and each has had a flagstone shelf. The chamber is open to the elements, its roof having been removed when the tomb was infilled in antiquity.

The site was excavated by its owner, a local farmer, Mr R. Simison. The north-end compartment and one of the side cells had been cleared before his excavations, but the remainder of the site yielded many human and animal remains, as well as Unstan pottery, bone and shell beads, stone implements and flints. The artefacts had been placed in groups on the floor rather than being mixed with the bones. The pottery, for example, was in a pile in the main chamber, opposite the entrance.

The human bones in the tomb represented 340 people. The skeletons were disarticulated and incomplete, and seemed to have been sorted into types of bones, many of the skulls for example, having been stored in two of the side-cells. John Hedges, the

*View along the main chamber, looking south-east, with the dividing slabs and the entrance into the east cell*

archaeologist associated with the project, noted that they looked 'as if they had been bowled in'. Some of the other bones were arranged in piles in the chamber, with more skulls along the side walls.

Unlike the animal bones in the tomb, the human bones were bleached and weathered, making it very probable that the bodies had been excarnated and defleshed before being gathered up and placed in the chamber. As there were no gnawing marks on the bones, Hedges suggested that the bodies had been laid out on mortuary platforms, exposed to the elements and birds of prey.

Because of the unusually large number of bones at Isbister, it was possible to study the Neolithic population using the tomb. The mixture of age and sex indicated that everyone had a right to burial in the tomb, rather than only segments of the community. Twenty four of the skeletons were of infants (under 2 years old), 70 of children (2–12 years), 63 of teenagers, and 185 over age 20. Of the adults, most died before they were 30, and 50 would have been considered exceptionally old.

Physically, the Isbister people were smaller than today's population. Men averaged 1.7m (5ft 7in) and women averaged 1.6m (5ft 3½in), but they were very muscular. The ailments and injuries which they suffered ranged from crushed vertebrae to abscesses in molar sockets, but by far the most common complaint was degenerative disease of the spine: at least 47 per cent of the population suffered from it.

*Looking south-west at the exterior wall of the cairn at Isbister, showing the hornworking at the entrance. On the left are the main chamber and the east cell*

Many animal, bird and fish bones were also found scattered on the floor of the chamber. Thirteen species of fish, two species of shellfish and 10 species of birds were identified. Of the animal bones, those of sheep were most common in the chamber, but cattle, pig and red deer were also present. These bones seemed to have been brought into the chamber as joints and left there; there are no butchery marks.

As has been mentioned, the tomb contained at least 10 carcasses of white-tailed sea eagle. Like the dog skulls at Cuween (*below*), they may have been a totem or emblem of the group which built the tomb. In some present-day societies, animals considered totems receive burial in the tombs.

# CUWEEN

On the north-east side of Cuween Hill, overlooking the Bay of Firth on Orkney Mainland, is a chambered tomb, known locally as the 'Fairy Knowe'.

The cairn was investigated in July 1901 by M.M. Charleson, who dug a trench across the top of the monument. Traces of a rectangular chamber appeared as the trench became deeper. Charleson recorded that they removed 'slabs of various sizes, earth and animal remains, among which the teeth of the dog were most conspicuous'. No pottery or flint was found, suggesting that the tomb might have been entered on a previous occasion.

The main chamber had a cell leading off each side, one of which was divided in two. In the earth covering the chamber floor, which Charleson described as having a 'fatty, unctious appearance', five human skulls and some human long bones were found. Two more skulls were discovered when the side cells were cleared out. One of them was found on a slab in a small recess built into the wall.

Twenty-four dog skulls had been placed on the chamber floor. Unfortunately there is nothing in the excavation report to say whether or not the breed was identified. The dogs may indicate the choice of a totem to protect the tribe, as has been suggested for the white-tailed eagles at Isbister (p. 100) and the red deer at Holm of Papa Westray North (p. 105). Another possibility is that the dog, unlike other domesticated animals, lived with a family, and was given similar burial rites to other family members.

*Main chamber of Cuween chambered tomb, showing the small entrances to two of the side cells, and part of the entrance to a third. Bedrock forms the floor*

# MIDHOWE

About 100m (330ft) south of the broch of Midhowe (p. 68) on the island of Rousay in Orkney, is Midhowe chambered tomb, a long stalled cairn. Before it was excavated, the site was a grassy mound 30m (100ft) long and 15m (50ft) broad, with a recent stone dyke running across the top. Since its excavation in 1932–3 it has been enclosed in a stone building.

The entrance, which is mid-way along the narrow south end, had been sealed with stone walling. The outer wall of the cairn had a foundation of slabs laid flat,

above which was a course of upright slabs set at an angle. The course above this was angled in the opposite direction, forming a herring-bone pattern.

At some point, the roof had been opened and the chamber filled with stony debris. When this was cleared out the chamber was found to comprise a long passage partitioned with sandstone slabs. It has been likened to a narrow byre with twelve stalls on each side.

The fifth to eleventh compartments on the north-east side of the chamber have low stone benches within them. The remains of 25 individuals – 17 adults and 6 younger persons (14–20 years old) had been placed on those shelves. Some of the bodies had been placed with their backs to the east wall, some with their heads to the north end, some with their heads to the south, but all

*Midhowe stalled cairn, looking south-east down the full length of the chamber to the passage. A modern stone building encloses the site*

*The blocked entrance at Midhowe cairn with the foundation layers of the exterior wall and the beginnings of the angled slabs above*

faced the passage. Only four heaps of bone were found under the shelves, and another three heaps on the chamber floor itself.

The condition of the bones indicated that, as at Isbister (p. 100), the bodies had been left to decompose before being brought into the tomb. In one cell, for example, the long-bones were piled up along the wall of the chamber with the skulls placed on top of them. The first four cells contained no bones and it is possible that they had a different purpose. The bodies may have been left there to rot before being moved to the other cells.

The average height of the people buried in Midhowe was less than of today's population. The tallest man was 1.6m (5ft 4in) and the smallest 1.5m (5ft 2in).

A study of the jaws showed that although there was no tooth decay, infection in the sockets had been a problem, and the crowns of some teeth were very worn. Overcrowding of teeth was also a problem, and one skull had impacted wisdom teeth. Of the three complete skulls found in the tomb, each had signs of osteo-arthritis in the mandible joint.

The pottery fragments recovered came from seven vessels, some of which were Unstan bowls. Most of the pottery was found in one of the cells near the middle of the passage. The only non-ceramic find associated with the Neolithic burials was a knife of brown flint.

At some point after the tomb went out of use, two bodies in the crouched position were buried in the rubble filling the chamber. There were also signs of later occupation on top of the mound. A passage was cleared from the north end at about 1m (3ft 3in) above the original floor level, and the breaking of the tops of the partitioning slabs in the chamber might have been done during an attempt to flatten an area of the rubble.

# UNSTAN

The chambered tomb of Unstan, on Orkney Mainland, is built on a promontory which juts out from the south shore of the Loch of Stenness.

Unstan tomb was excavated in 1884 by R.S. Clouston, an Orkney antiquarian. The site is famous for its pottery, wide shallow bowls, with deep 'collars', the remains of about 35 being found. Some of the collars were decorated with various patterns, most based on a triangular theme. Since the Unstan excavations, similar shallow bowls have been found at many other funerary sites and some domestic sites and the pottery is now known as Unstan ware.

At Unstan, the cairn was constructed of concentric rings of walling. The chamber is long and was subdivided into five compartments, in each of which were found skeletal remains. The two end compartments have stones projecting from the side walls, presumably to support shelves. A small side-chamber leading off the passage housed two crouched burials.

In addition to the human bones, many bird and animal bones were found, also a stone pounder, and several flint tools which had been burnt before their deposition in the tomb.

*The main chamber of Unstan, looking south. The end compartment has a kerb between the projecting slabs and its end wall is formed of a slab with stone walling above*

# HOLM OF PAPA WESTRAY SOUTH

The Holm of Papa Westray, a small island in the Orkney islands, was probably once a promontory of the larger island of Papa Westray. The archaeology suggests that in Neolithic times at least, the Holm of Papa Westray supported a lively farming community.

Two chambered tombs have been excavated on the island – a cairn of 'Maes Howe' type (the South cairn) and a stalled cairn (the North cairn).

The South cairn was excavated in 1849 by a Captain Thomas. At the time of the excavation most archaeological mounds were termed 'Pict's Houses'. Captain Thomas thought this was what he had uncovered:

> When speculating upon the probable use of this extraordinary structure, it must be borne in mind that it is situated most conspicuously upon the highest part of a very small island; it could not therefore have been intended either for concealment or defence as nothing would have been easier than to have buried the inmates in the ruins of their hiding place: the most reasonable supposition is that they were the temporary habitations of a nomade people.

On excavation, the mound of the tomb was found to be surrounded by a low stone wall, an outer casing. The walling along the entrance passage was smooth, and the passage roof was of large flagstones.

Although the passageway is still complete, visitors to the tomb now enter the chamber down a ladder, through a hatch in the roof. The chamber is elongated and has a subdividing wall with a low doorway at each end. Twelve small entrances lead off the chamber – three on each side of the main part of the chamber, and three (one in each wall) in each of the subdivided end portions. Ten of these entrances lead to a small cell, and two lead to a double cell, making 14 cells in all.

The finds from the tomb were disappointing, comprising a few bones of sheep and rabbits, thought from their condition to be recent. However, Thomas found that various stones in the chamber wall were decorated. The motifs included zig-zags and inverted v's (also found on pottery), and dots and arcs, sometimes put together to form 'eyebrows'. These eyebrow motifs have also been found on the walls of some Irish tombs. It is possible that some motifs had ritual significance, being repeated on pottery used in various ceremonies and on chamber walls, and perhaps also being painted on those taking part in the rituals.

At the north of the Holm of Papa Westray is the stalled cairn already mentioned. It was excavated in 1854 by George Petrie and more recently by Anna Ritchie, who also excavated Knap of Howar, a domestic site on Papa Westray (p. 23). A great variety of animal and bird bones were recovered, fish bones and deer antlers predominating. Deer and fish may have been totems of the tribe who built the tomb. Alternatively, the remains may represent a food offering to the gods. It is possible that only certain foods (varying from tribe to tribe) were considered suitable as offerings.

Anna Ritchie pointed out the similarities between the plans of the homestead of Knap of Howar, and the tombs on the Holm of Papa Westray. Although it is possible that the similarities were due to the builders using familiar techniques for both types of site, the possibility remains that the planning was deliberate, the tombs being thought of as the 'houses' of the dead.

*Interior of Holm of Papa Westray South, showing cell entrances leading off the main chamber*

*The lintel above the entrance to one of the side cells, decorated with incised 'eyebrow' motifs and dots*

# THE DWARFIE STANE

In the remote glen between the Ward Hill and the Dwarfie Hamars, on the Orkney island of Hoy lies a large sandstone block which has fallen from the rocky scarps above.

The Norse settlers named the stone 'Dvergasteinn', or the 'Dwarfie Stane', and it has been known locally by this name ever since. In Norse mythology the dwarfs were skilled smiths who lived in hollowed-out boulders or in hillsides. In reality, the stone is a rock-cut tomb,

*The Dwarfie Stane, looking north-east, with the entrance, and the blocking stone. The cross-bedding of the sandstone shows clearly on the front of the tomb*

thought to belong to the Neolithic period, although nothing is known of what it contained.

The stone, which measures 8.5 by 4.5 by 2m (28 by 15 by 6ft 6in), has a rock-cut passage off which lead two cells, one on each side. Each cell has a kerb separating it from the passage. In the cell on the right of the passage, a step or 'pillow' of rock has been left at one end. A large stone lying in front of the tomb was used to block the entrance. There is a hole in the ceiling which may have been made during attempts to lever the stone out of its original position. The only similar site in the British Isles is St Kevin's Bed, at Glendalough, in the Wicklow Mountains, south of Dublin.

Apart from being such an unusual site, the Dwarfie

*The passage inside the Dwarfie Stane, showing the raised lips into each chamber, and the stone 'pillow' in the cell on the right*

Stane is well known for its mention in Sir Walter Scott's novel *The Pirate*, where it is described by Norna of Fitful Head as the 'favourite residence' of Trolld, a dwarf mentioned in the Northern Sagas.

The earliest reference to the site was by Jo Ben who wrote a description of Orkney in the early sixteenth century. His tale was that the chambers were hewn out by a giant and his pregnant wife. The blocking stone had its place in the tale too. It was said to have been thrown there by another giant, who, jealous of the rock-cut home, had hurled the stone from the mountain side hoping to trap the giant and his wife inside, leaving them there to starve to death. The giant inside the tomb had to break a hole in the roof in order to get out.

Some of the many visitors to the stone have carved their names on its faces. On the southern exterior is carved 'Guilemus Mounsey', reading from right to left, and the date AD 1850. The signature is that of a major in the Indian Army, who had been a British Spy in Persia and Afghanistan. He had visited Hoy, and stayed for several days in the Dwarfie Stane. The Major was said to be a strange looking chap with a beard and yellow Persian shoes, and the locals thought he was a 'mad jew' who had taken possession of the stone. A few lines of poetry written in Persian underneath his signature translate as 'Oh God: I am pierced to the heart, and very sorrowful, I wake all night, and study and learn patience'. The poetry is thought to refer to a swarm of midges which had come into the stone during his stay.

# TAVERSOE TUICK

In the summer of 1898, General Frederick William Traill-Burroughs and Lady Burroughs of Trumland House on Rousay, Orkney, decided to cut a summer seat into a small heather-covered knoll known locally as Taversoe Tuick.

The workmen were summoned and instructed to dig a wedge out of the side of the hillock. By the middle of the afternoon it was obvious that the section being removed was too small and the decision was taken to enlarge it. Shortly afterwards the remains of several 'cists' were discovered. Lady Burroughs recorded the event in her journal:

> It was now about 5 pm. Munro's face was dark, the Inhabitants don't much like finding these burials. A Stone rather larger than the rest was raised; there was a fall of earth; and to our wondering eyes a huge stone Lintel appeared, a broken one beside it, underneath which we got a glimpse of a dark gloomy underground chamber, these Lintels forming the roof. We were all breathless! a sharp clap of thunder at the moment completed the weird scene . . . I went to the Mound that afternoon carrying a basket full of spring flowers to plant at the Summer seat. On the homeward journey my basket contained a Skull.

*Taversoe Tuick, looking north-east, and showing the modern dome covering the upper chamber, and the entrance to the lower chamber. In the foreground is the miniature chamber*

*Interior of lower chamber, showing two of the four compartments and shelving, with the entrance passage to the left. The roof forms the floor of the upper chamber*

The tomb which Lady Burroughs and her workmen uncovered was one of only two double-storeyed cairns known – the other is Huntersquoy on the island of Eday. The diameter of the cairn is about 9m (30ft) but there is a platform of flat stones covering an area roughly 3 by 7m (10 by 23ft) to the south of it.

There was no access from one chamber to the other: instead they were built as two tombs, one above the other, with individual entrance passages. The arrangement is possible because the tomb is built on a slope, the lower of the two chambers being cut into the bedrock.

Originally a paved entrance passage on the south led to the lower chamber which is divided into four compartments by upright slabs. Each compartment had flagstone shelving to hold skeletal remains, and piles of bones, including a crouched burial, were found. There were more remains, this time cremated, in the passage. The walls of the lower chamber were of drystone, built up the side of the cut bedrock, and the lintels forming the roof (which was also the floor of the upper chamber) rest not on this masonry, but on the bedrock behind.

Diametrically opposite the entrance to the lower chamber is the entrance to the upper chamber. This chamber is divided in two, and the skeletal remains comprised the cremated bones of a child and several adults in three stone cists, covered by slabs.

In addition to the 'double' cairn, there was a smaller chamber dug into the ground about 7m (23ft) from it. This 'miniature cairn' which measures only 1.5 by 1.3m (5 by 4ft) had a lintelled roof, and was divided into five narrow bays by four slabs. Inside were found three pottery bowls, almost complete, but no skeletal remains. It has been suggested that this cairn may have had a different use, perhaps connected with ritual – a place to leave food and drink offerings.

# PUNDS WATER

Built on a hillock in the rolling heathery moorland near Mangaster on Shetland Mainland is Punds Water cairn. The large white quartzite boulders of the tomb stand out from the surrounding barren countryside.

The tomb is a heel-shaped cairn, one of a group unique to Shetland and first identified by the Royal Commission, during work for the Shetland Inventory in the 1930s. The sites were described as having, in addition to a heel-shaped plan, a chamber with a trefoil outline. These cairns are small – Punds Water is one of the largest of the group, having a diameter of only 15m (50ft).

The 'back' of the tomb is rounded, the walls spreading out towards the front, forming the two horns of a rounded facade.

A narrow entrance passage 4m (13ft) long leads from the centre of the facade to the chamber. The largest of the recesses faced the entrance, with a smaller one to the left and right. When the chamber was cleared out in 1930, it was found to have a clay floor with red water-rolled pebbles embedded into it. The pebbles had probably been brought from some distance away.

*Punds Water cairn, looking north-west. The cairn is situated between two of the Shetland's many lochs, Punds Water and Mina Water*

# CAMSTER

Near Watten in Caithness, two massive mounds of grey boulders, one round and 18m (60ft) in diameter, the other long and stretching nearly 70m (230ft), rise conspicuously from the bleak, open moorland. These chambered cairns are within 200m (650ft) of each other, and are striking in their shape contrasts.

Restoration work to the monuments has made entry to their interior chambers as easy as possible through the long and narrow passages. Anderson and Shearer who explored the sites in 1865 for the Anthropological Society of London, entered the chamber of the round cairn by less conventional means. They lowered themselves into the chamber from the top of the cairn where one of the capstones had given way. The chamber was filled with loose stones which had rolled in from the mound above, and these had to be cleared before any further progress could be made.

As they cleared out the stones, Anderson and Shearer located the position of the doorway to the passage leading to the side of the mound. The passageway itself was tightly packed with stones from floor to roof and from end to end. As the flags forming the roof were closely set and intact, the excavators concluded that the filling had been deliberate.

There could be various reasons for the final blocking of a communal tomb. The chamber may have received its allotted number of burials, or the final burial might have seen the end of a family line. If the families using the tomb were moving on to another area, they may have sealed their tomb to stop other groups from using or disturbing it. Alternatively, the tomb could have been sealed by newcomers to the area in an attempt to

*Camster Long cairn showing the restored horned forecourt and the entrance to the passage*

*Looking from the chamber of Camster Round cairn,
though the portal stones towards the antechamber*

lock the spirits of the previous inhabitants safely in the heart of the mound.

At Camster Round, the skulls and upper bones of two skeletons were found among the stones blocking the passage. The bones had not been laid on the floor, but were among the boulders above it. Anderson and Shearer suggested that the bodies had been placed on the wet earth of the passage in a sitting position with the stones packed around them. This could explain the absence of bones from the lower part of the skeleton – those bones in contact with the wet ground would have been quicker to decay.

The finds from the chamber itself were scanty. More bone fragments, some animal, but most human, were recovered from the black earthy clay on the floor. Mixed in with the bones were large quantities of ash and charcoal, although few of the bones were burnt. There were fragments of two types of pottery vessel, one large and thick, the other small and very thin.

The decoration included incised lines, finger-tip impressions and dots possibly made with the end of a quill. Various flint implements including an arrowhead and a flint knife were also discovered.

In the year following these excavations, Anderson and Shearer investigated Camster Round's neighbour, Camster Long. The finds were similar to those from the chamber of Camster Round – mainly broken and charred animal and human bone. However, it is the structure rather than the finds which is important in this case.

The cairn has short 'horns' forming forecourts at each end. In long cairns, the entrance to the passage leading to the chamber is usually located in the forecourt, but at

*The entrance passage at Camster Long cairn, looking from the north-east chamber*

Camster Long the two burial chambers are entered from the side of the mound. One of the chambers is a simple polygonal chamber, but the other is more complex, and pairs of slabs projecting from the wall divide off the passage from the antechamber, and the antechamber from the chamber. As well as providing compartments, this architectural development also reduces the roof span.

Recent excavations of the mound, completed in 1980, revealed why the entrances were not aligned with the forecourt. The reason is an interesting one; the chambers originally belonged to two separate round cairns. The addition of the long mound, enveloping the cairns, was a later venture.

The length of a long cairn is seldom due to the number of chambers which it houses. At Camster Long, the massive mound housed only two small chambers. A great deal of effort would have been expended in the transportation of the material to build the mound over the two existing cairns. As the burial capacity was not increased by the building of the mound, the mound itself must have been important to the status of the community which built it. Seen from a distance, it would have indicated their power and importance to outsiders. For the perhaps scattered community which erected and maintained it, the mound would have been a focus of ritual activity and a monument to the gods and ancestors, rather than a purely functional burial vault.

*Camster Round cairn, showing the entrance facade, with the Caithness moorland stretching off in the distance*

# GARRYWHIN (CAIRN OF GET)

In a hollow in the Caithness moorland between the north end of Groat's Loch and Broughwhin, lies a short horned cairn now covered with turf and heather. It was excavated in 1866 by Anderson and Shearer, who also excavated at Camster (p. 111). There were signs that the tomb had been disturbed and robbed previous to these excavations.

To the tips of the horns, the cairn is about 25m (80ft) long. The excavators found that there had been two wall faces defining the outline of the cairn, and also one surrounding the chamber. These walls would have helped contain the spread of the boulder mound.

The 3m (11ft) long passage was entered between two low stones, placed only 0.8m (2ft 6in) apart. The passage only increased slightly in width towards the chamber. It is not certain whether the passage was

*Garrywhin, looking north, with the entrance passage and the grass-covered horns of the facade*

roofed with lintels or by corbelling, because it was roofless even at the time of the excavations.

The chamber itself is divided by two large irregularly shaped slabs. The outer part is rectangular, and the inner part more rounded. Each of the walls in the inner chamber is formed of a slab of sandstone, with walling built up around it. Further up the wall, the beginnings of corbelling can be made out.

Both burnt and unburnt flint were recovered from the chamber. There were many flint flakes, and also two or three leaf-shaped arrowheads. The many pottery sherds were from well-made, hard-fired vessels. Although the finds are now lost, Anderson recorded that some sherds had come from round-bottomed vessels, and that most of them were undecorated, the only decoration being finger-nail indentations.

Anderson described the deposit in the chamber in this way:

*Garrywhin, looking from the antechamber into the chamber, through the portals. The back wall is formed of a slab surrounded by drystone*

On the floor of the main compartment of the chamber there was the largest accumulation of ashes, mixed with bones, burnt and unburnt, and pottery, that we have found in any of the cairns. In the centre it formed a compact mass of about eighteen inches in thickness. We examined it most carefully as it was lifted, and found it plentifully mixed with wood ashes and charcoal, many of the fragments indicating pieces of wood of considerable thickness.

The fact that the compacted deposit in the chamber contained a mixture of burnt and unburnt bones, artefacts and ash, suggested that it may have been the remains of funeral pyres, feasting, or sacrifice. The burning would have been carried out on a pyre outside. Henshall has suggested an alternative explanation, that the burnt layer represents burning of the bones once they were in the chamber, by a 'cleansing' fire brought in to the tomb as glowing charcoal.

On top of the burnt layer in the outer chamber were the remains of seven or eight unburnt skeletons, which Anderson thought may have been indicative of a change in funerary rites. He noted that the skulls were all to the right side of the entrance, as if the bodies had been laid across the doorway, but the size of the chamber makes this unlikely. There were bones on the burnt layer of the inner chamber too, both from adults and young children.

# CNOC FREICEADAIN

Near the summit of Cnoc Freiceadain, Caithness, are two grass-covered horned long cairns, set at right angles to each other. The mounds are low for much of their length, having been victim to stone robbing. The most obvious features of the site are three round mounds which led to the sites being named 'Na Tri Shean' (the three fairy mounds) by the locals. Although the mounds have not been excavated, one theory is that three separate cairns were incorporated into two long mounds.

Horns defining forecourts can be made out at the northern end of the north cairn, and at both ends of the south cairn. At 71m (230ft), the south cairn is one of the largest known.

Above *The northern cairn with the mound tailing off to the left*

Below *Looking north-west along the southern cairn which is now surrounded by Caithness slab fences. In the background is Dounreay with the Pentland Firth beyond*

# COILLE NA BORGIE

On a moorland terrace above the River Naver near Rhinavie in Sutherland, the two horned long cairns, Coille na Borgie North and South, lie end to end. When the cairns were first described in the archaeological literature in the nineteenth century, it was thought that there were three cairns rather than two, but it was later realised that the northern two were actually one cairn cut by a cart track.

Both cairns are orientated north to south, separated by less than 10m (33ft). The north cairn measures 57m (190ft) including the horns, while the south cairn measures 72m (235ft). At each end of the cairns is a horned facade, with the longer pair of horns oriented to the north, and the shorter pair to the south. The entrance to each opened from the middle of the larger facade. Nineteenth-century investigations have damaged the structure of the chambers and passageways.

The mounds themselves were made of large rounded boulders, probably from the river. The facades were marked out by some larger upright slabs. The facade stones of the southern cairn were biggest at the ends of the horns, decreasing in size towards the entrance.

When the tomb was investigated, very few finds were recorded, only some pieces of charred wood and animal bone in the chamber of the southern cairn.

*Coille na Borgie chambered cairns, looking north over the chamber and forecourt of the southern cairn, with the northern cairn beyond. The River Naver is visible below*

# MUTINY STONES

High in the Lammermuir Hills, overlooking the Dye Water, is a long cairn, the Mutiny Stones. The origin of the name is a mystery, but 'Mutiny' may be a corruption of the older name 'Mitten o'Stanes'. Local legend has it that the devil was carrying stones, wrapped in his mitten, from Dunbar to Kelso to build a dam across the Tweed, when his mitten burst and the stones tumbled out onto the hillside.

Excavations in 1871, organised by a local resident Lady John Scott revealed little. Lady Scott's sister wrote about the day in her diary:

*The Mutiny Stones in the moorland of the Lammermuir Hills. A sheep fank has been built into the mound using some of the cairn stones*

Monday, July 10, 1871. In spite of the weather, we went to Byrecleugh. It was a perfect downpour, so we sat in the carriage, while the men moved the stones according to Dr. Stuart's directions. After luncheon it cleared, and we took a walk to see some other stones of which Dr. Stuart did not think much and then returned to the Mitten, where by this time they had got down a considerable distance under the cairn, without however coming to anything.

Further excavations in 1924 by the Berwickshire Naturalists' Club added little. All that was discovered was a section of walling within the mound which may have represented the remains of a chamber opening from the side of the cairn.

# CAPO

In a clearing in the pines of Inglismaldie forest, Kincardine and Deeside, is an earthen long barrow, one of few surviving in Scotland. It is 80m (260ft) long, 25m (80ft) wide at its wider east end, and 2.5m (8ft) high. The mound was constructed of turfs and earth, with a drystone wall revetting it, although it is now grass-covered.

Earthen long barrows are more common south of the border than in Scotland. In Neolithic Scotland long cairns with stone mounds were more common. Where excavations have been carried out, it has been found that the burials were in the broader, usually east end of the mound, in a 'mortuary house' constructed of turf, stone or timber, or a combination of these.

Excavations at the earthen long barrow at Dalladies in Kincardineshire uncovered a mortuary house with different phases of building in stone and timber, and the mortuary house under the barrow at Lochhill in Kirkcudbrightshire, had been built with both split timbers and granite boulders. As with long cairns, the size of the mound was far in excess of what was required to cover the mortuary house.

At both Dalladies and Lochhill, there were traces of timber facades in front of the Mortuary houses which had been burnt before the mounds were built over the remains. The mound at Dalladies was used later for burials – stone cists and settings had been dug into it.

*Capo earthen long barrow in its wooded surroundings. It was built on the edge of a natural terrace above the River Esk which is below the barrow on the far side*

# RUDH' AN DUNAIN

On a windswept peninsula of Skye, with the Cuillin Hills and the islands of Eigg and Rhum as backdrops, is the chambered cairn of Rudh' an Dunain. It was excavated in 1931 and 1932 by Sir Lindsay and Mrs Scott. The monument shows many of the features of the class of 'Hebridean tombs' to which it belongs.

Before excavation, the site was covered in rough grass and heather and was slightly higher than its present 3.5m (11ft 6in). Sir Lindsay and Mrs Scott excavated the chamber from the top downwards. In his excavation report, Sir Lindsay commented on the difficulties which they had encountered. No local labour had been available, and the only equipment which the couple had was a short length of chain, some grass rope, and some large driftwood from the shore. Any stones which were too heavy to be pushed up the makeshift wooden ramp had to be levered on round pebbles. It was strenuous work – some of the stones such as the roof slabs each weighed more than half a ton.

When the chamber was eventually cleared, it was found to be polygonal in shape, and built, as Sir Lindsay described it 'on the principle of half timbering with alternate orthostatic pillars and panels of drystone masonry'. The orthostats stood on the rock floor, and were not wedged at their bases. Most of the drystone courses were formed from a single slab, lessening the chance of the panels buckling. The horizontal pressure of the cairn gave the chamber wall its stability.

*Right Rudh' an Dunain chambered cairn, looking from the chamber outwards through the antechamber and vestibule to the entrance. Note the decreasing height of the roof*

In the construction of the chamber, the builders had used orthostats of locally available igneous rocks – basalt, gabbro and dolerite. The roof was not corbelled, but was formed of basalt slabs, as was the roofing of the antechamber and vestibule which led out to the facade. The roof of the vestibule was lower than that of the antechamber which in turn was lower than the chamber roof.

The tomb was edged with a peristalith of orthostats a metre apart, with drystone walling between, but this is obscured to some extent due to slippage of the cairn material. Like the peristalith, the forecourt was constructed of orthstats with walling between. Although many of the orthostats have been pushed out of their original position by the weight of the cairn, it is still possible to see that their height decreased from the portal outwards.

Two different groups used the tomb for the burial of their dead. Fragments of pottery of the Neolithic group who built the tomb were found in the lower levels of the chamber. The fragments were from open-necked bowls with vertical sides and turned-over rims.

Unfortunately, the bones did not survive well. Some

*Detail of the chamber post and panel walling in the chamber of Rudh' an Dunain*

*The entrance, facade and forecourt at Rudh' an Dunain. The orthostats have been dislodged by slippage of the cairn material*

were human (a middle-aged individual, probably male), some animal, and some bird. A lozenge-shaped quartz tool and two flint scrapers were also found.

When the chamber was built, a foundation deposit of bone (too decayed to be identified as either animal or human) had been made at the foot of one of the orthostats. This may have been an offering to the guardian of the tomb.

Later the tomb was used by an early Bronze Age group. This time, the pottery associated with the human remains was a beaker decorated with two bands of diagonal decoration. The bone fragments were identified as a young man, a 30–35 year-old person, probably male, and two young adults, one aged 18–20.

# UNIVAL

The remains of the chambered tomb of Unival stand on an isolated hill looking over the scatter of lochs in the central plain of North Uist.

Due to stone robbing, the most obvious features of this Hebridean tomb are the orthostats which formed parts of the facade, antechamber and chamber walls.

Sir Lindsay Scott who excavated Rudh' an Dunain chambered tomb (p. 120) on Skye, investigated Unival in the 1930s. Inside the chamber he found a stone slab cist built in one corner. It contained the burnt bone fragments of an adult woman. Although burnt they were not cremated – it seemed that hot charcoal had been put over them. Sir Lindsay suggested that this was to drive the ghost from the decomposed body.

Fragments of several pottery bowls were found in the cist and on the chamber floor. Piles of bones and pottery around the walls of the chamber suggest that the contents of the cist were emptied between burials.

The chamber was used many years after the final Neolithic burial. By this time the cist was full of earth which had filtered through the roof. As the floor level of the antechamber was now too high to allow a body to be brought into the chamber, the capstone would have been removed and the corpse lowered through the roof.

*The orthostats of the denuded cairn at Unival. To the right of the orthostats is the outline of the foundations of an Iron Age house*

# VATTEN

Overlooking Loch Caroy on Skye, are a pair of Hebridean cairns. It is probable that each cairn was built on a low platform edged by a kerb, although slipped mound material on the southern cairn obscures any traces of a platform.

As the mounds have not been excavated, it is unclear why the two were built together, but local folklore provides its own interpretations.

One tale is that one of the mounds is the burial place of a great chief who owned the surrounding land. Each summer he went on a raiding mission with his men, bringing back gold, cattle and slaves. One summer he did not return when expected, but in the autumn the ships sailed slowly into the bay. The body of the chief was carried ashore on his men's shields to be buried in a huge grave, while in the bay below, his galley was ritually set alight.

Another legend holds that the mounds are built on the site of the last battle between the Macdonalds and the MacLeods, two rival clans in Skye. A thick mist descended during the fighting, resulting in carnage so complete that only women and old men were left to bury the dead. All that could be done was to make two piles of bodies, one for each clan, and cover them with stones.

*The chambered cairns at Vatten with Loch Caroy and the Cuillin Hills in the background*

# BALNUARAN OF CLAVA

At Balnuaran of Clava, near Inverness, is a line of three cairns, each surrounded by a circle of standing stones. The cairns are variations on the same design. The central one in the line is a 'Clava' ring cairn, and the other two, known as the North-East and the South-West cairns are 'Clava' passage graves. All the cairns have an outer kerb and an inner chamber built of large stones. The difference between the two groups is that the passage graves have, as their name suggests, a passage running from the kerb to the chamber.

Clava cairns are found mainly in the area around Inverness and the Black Isle, and the Spey Valley. Their distribution coincides largely with areas of good farmland, and often the smaller stones of the mounds have been almost totally removed for the construction of dykes and farm buildings. This was being done as early as the eighteenth century. Records often refer to the concentric circles of slab kerbing that were left as 'Druid's Circles', and frequently compared them with Stonehenge.

Dr Johnson and James Boswell visited one of these 'Druid's Circles' during their tour of the Highlands in 1773. Boswell records:

> About three miles beyond Inverness, we saw, just by the road, a very complete specimen of what is called a Druid's temple. There was a double circle, one of very large, the other of smaller stones.
> Dr. Johnson justly observed that 'to go and see one druidical temple is only to see that it is nothing,

*Looking southwards over the chamber and passage of the North-East passage grave. In the background are the ring-cairn and the South-West passage grave*

*The cup-marked boulder in the kerb of the North-East cairn*

for there is neither art nor power in it; and seeing one is quite enough'.

All three cairns at Balnuaran of Clava have been excavated or 'investigated' at one time or another, but still retain most of their stone cairns. We know that the cairns were 'restored' by the owner of the land in 1881, when their roofing was removed.

Stuart Piggott excavated the ring cairn in 1953. It was constructed as a thick doughnut of stones about 18m (60ft) in diameter. The loose cairn stones were held in place by a kerb of massive boulders on the outside, and a ring of upright slabs on the inside. A low platform of cairn material on the exterior kept the kerb stones in place. It is assumed that the central space was covered over once a burial had been made, as the cairn has no passage. Two slabs in the central area appeared to be the remains of a cist which had been destroyed previously.

Around the cairn was an orthostat circle. Three of the nine stones were 'attached' to the kerb of the cairn by radiating causeways or banks, likened by Piggott to the spokes of a wheel. Their function is not known. Only a few fragments of cremated bone were recovered during the excavations.

*Looking west at the ring cairn, showing the kerb and two stones of the surrounding circle. The stone in the foreground is 'joined' to the kerb by a low bank*

As has been mentioned, the two passage graves were very similar in plan to the ring cairn, apart from having passages. The passages and chambers were probably partially corbelled and then roofed with slabs. The entrances to the passages face south-west, pointing in the directon of the mid-winter sunset. This is a trait of the Clava passage graves as a whole. In general, the entrances to most chambered tombs face in an easterly direction.

The North-East passage grave at Balnuaran of Clava is surrounded by a boulder kerb with a diameter of 17m (55ft). The cairn material extended in a platform beyond the kerb stones. The boulders in the kerb are largest nearest the entrance, and decrease in size towards

*The remains of a small Bronze Age kerb cairn. There are cup marks on one of the boulders to the left*

*The South-West passage grave, looking north with two of the surrounding stones in the background*

the back of the cairn. The passage walls are made of boulders and sandstone slabs. Like the passage, the central chamber, which is only 4m (13 ft) in diameter, is also formed of upright boulders and slabs, for its lower course. All that was found in the chamber were a few bones.

The South-West cairn is very similar to the North-East cairn, although the platform and the stone circle have been damaged by the construction of a road. Both passage graves have cup-marked stones. The North-East cairn has a cup-marked stone in its kerb, and another in the passage, while the South-West cairn has cup marks on one of the boulders in the wall of the chamber.

Both cremations and inhumations have been found in Clava passage graves, and cremations in the ring cairns. From the limited evidence available, it seems that the Clava cairns were not burial places of whole communities, but of selected individuals, both males and females.

To the west of the central cairn is a small ring of boulders just 3.7m (12ft) in diameter, probably evidence of further use of the site in the late Bronze Age.

# CORRIMONY

On a flood-plain of the River Enrick, in Glen Urquhart, are the remains of a cairn 20m (65ft) in diameter, surrounded by a ring of eleven standing stones, known in the area as the Druid's Circle.

Before it was excavated by Stuart Piggott in 1952, this 'Clava' cairn appeared untouched, but this was not the case. A large cup-marked stone which lay on the summit of the cairn had probably been the capstone of the burial chamber. The chamber had been broken into, probably in the nineteenth century (fragments of nineteenth century china and glass were found mixed with the fill). The capstone was replaced on the top of the cairn after the backfilling.

The stone circle had also been tampered with. Plans

drawn in 1874 and 1882 showed nine stones in the circle, not eleven. Two of the standing stones in the circle had been made up of several unconnected slabs, probably roofing slabs from the passage.

The stones used in the construction of the site could all have been obtained locally. The cairn, for example, was made of water-worn boulders from the River Enrick. The lower part of the cairn had been formed of larger boulders than the upper part. Around the cairn was a kerb of about 45 slabs, the largest near the entrance. The slabs had originally stood upright, but had been forced outwards by the weight of the mound material.

Cairn material extended outside the kerb for about 2m (7ft), forming a platform which would have held the kerbstones in place. All around the kerbstones were hundreds of broken pieces of white quartz which had been scattered when the tomb was being built.

*Looking north-west at Corrimony chambered cairn, with some of the stones in its surrounding circle of orthostats*

*The chamber of Corrimony cairn. To the left is the cup-marked stone which may have formed the capstone, and in the background is part of the stone circle*

The only artefact recovered during the excavations was a rough bone pin, which was found among the drystone blocking of the entrance passage. The walls of the entrance passage were formed of large uprights. Seven metres (23ft) into the cairn, the passage opened into the chamber. Its wall was formed of fifteen stone blocks arranged in a circle with corbelled walling above.

Although the chamber had been opened previously, the stones covering the floor had not been removed until Piggott's excavations. They were found to overlay a floor of yellow sand. In the centre of the floor was some charcoal, and an area paved with flat stone slabs. When the sand was scraped clean, a stained area was revealed. The following description was given in the excavation report:

> a series of strongly marked grey, purplish–black and white stains in this region formed identifiable outlines which could be interpreted as those of a crouched inhumation burial, with its skull particularly well defined, lying on its right side with its head towards the north west.

Phosphate enrichment of the soil confirmed the visuals – a body had been buried in the chamber, laid directly on the natural sand.

# NETHER LARGIE AND RI CRUIN

In the Kilmartin Valley in Argyll, is a line of cairns including a chambered round cairn and two cairns covering cists. They are known as Nether Largie North, Mid and South and are part of a large complex of standing stones, tombs and carved stones which tell something of the ritual life of the community from the Neolithic to the later Bronze Age. It is thought the cairns may be the successive burials of a ruling family or chieftains.

The oldest burial site is the chambered round cairn Nether Largie South. It is a Clyde cairn and is built on the valley floor, near the centre of the line of tombs. The cairn was 'excavated' by Canon Greenwell over three days in October 1864, during a two week expedition of cairn opening in the west of Scotland.

Nether Largie South had a diameter of over 40m (130ft) which includes a platform or extension to the

*Nether Largie Mid cairn with the southern cist in the foreground. In the background are Nether Largie North cairn and the Glebe cairn*

*The segmented chamber of Nether Largie South chambered cairn. The floor level is much higher than it was originally*

original cairn. By the time Greenwell examined it, most of the cairn material had already been removed. The mound covered two cists as well as the central chamber.

The central chamber was entered from the north. It is oblong, about 6 by 1.2m (20 by 4ft), constructed of schist slabs and drystone walling. The floor was divided into four by three slabs which now only project a little above the present floor level, although Greenwell recorded them as being 0.8m (2ft 6in) in height. The chamber is roofed with large slabs, about 2.8m (9ft) above the original floor.

In the inner two compartments Greenwell found a pavement of dark earth and pebbles, with cremated bone and quartz flakes mixed through it. On top of the earth layer, in one corner of the inner compartment, was a cist made from six stone slabs. Nothing was found inside the cist, but the remains of some beakers and several inhumation burials were found near it.

The two cists in the surrounding platform had been uncovered before Greenwell's investigations. Only one is now visible. One cist was empty, the other contained a food vessel.

The two cairns north of Nether Largie South, Nether Largie Mid and North, had no chambers, only cists. Nether Largie Mid cairn was excavated in 1929. Two cists were found within the 30m (100ft) diameter cairn.

*Nether Largie South showing the entrance and capstones, with the x setting of five standing stones near Temple Wood (p. 150) in the background*

The northern cist had been formed of slabs, those at the sides grooved so that the end slabs would slot in neatly. Nothing remains of the cist, but its position is marked by four concrete posts. The other cist has survived, and is displayed with its capstone propped open on steel supports. It was also empty when excavated, but on its northern end slab a single cup mark and an axe carving were found.

Nether Largie North cairn covered only one central cist. One tooth, some ochre (perhaps body paint) and a little charcoal was all that was found on its excavation in 1930. The slabs of the cist made up for the lack of grave goods. One end slab was decorated with representations of two axe heads, while at least 10 axeheads and 40 cup-marks were carved on the underside of the capstone. The cist can now be viewed by descending into the centre of the cairn through a hatch, which leads to a viewing chamber.

Aubrey Burl has suggested that axe carvings, along with some bronze and even chalk axes placed in 'ceremonial' situations, indicate 'rituals in which axes were raised to the skies in honour of the dead and in salutation to their spirits'.

North of Nether Largie North cairn is another cairn, known as the Glebe cairn. The central cist contained an inhumation burial and a food vessel. Another food vessel was found with a further inhumation burial and the beads from a jet necklace in a second cist.

*Nether Largie North cairn. The cist and its carved capstone which before preservation was covered with cairn material*

*Ri Cruin cairn with the northern cist in the foreground. The cist at the edge of the cairn is that decorated with the axe carvings*

Also located in the Kilmartin Valley near Temple Wood stone circle (p. 150) is Ri Cruin cairn. Like most of the other cairns in the area it has a low stone mound covering stone cists, three in this case. Some of the cist slabs are grooved and rebated. The southern cist has axe carvings on it, and, carving which could be interpreted as a boat, perhaps, as Burl suggests, a vessel to carry the dead to the other world.

# CAIRNHOLY *I* AND *II*

On a hillside overlooking Wigtown Bay are the eerie skeletons of two chambered tombs. Although much of the cairn material has been removed, the larger stones of the monuments have been left in place.

Cairnholy I and II are 'Clyde' cairns. As a group, these cairns are usually trapezoidal in shape with the main chamber leading from the wider 'front' end of the cairn which sometimes has a forecourt and often has a facade of upright stones. Some tombs have further chambers opening from other sides of the mound. Cairnholy I and II deviate slightly from the 'classic' style of Clyde cairn.

Cairnholy I was originally 43m (140ft) long and 10m (33ft) wide, with straight sides. The tomb was an obvious source of stone for local builders, and the substantial stone dykes of the surrounding fields are likely to have been built of stones from the mound.

At the east end of the cairn was a crescent-shaped forecourt, with a facade of eight asymmetrically arranged stones, the two at the centre forming portal stones leading to the chamber. The plan of the slab-built chamber was a surprise to the excavators, Piggott and Powell. A high upright slab blocked access from the

*Below The facade of Cairnholy 1 chambered cairn with the sloping narrow portal stones in the centre.*

*Right The capstone and portal stones of Cairnholy II chambered cairn, surrounded by the remains of the mound, now turf-covered*

antechamber to the main chamber. Entry to the main chamber must have been from above, before the capstone was added.

On excavation, the top part of the antechamber was found to be full of earth and stones. Below this rubble were two layers of paving 0.2m (8in) apart, with earth mixed with pieces of bone and pottery between. The chamber itself had already been dug into, and there was little to find apart from a cup-and-ring marked stone, propped up against the wall. Sherds of a food vessel were also found in the chamber, making it likely that the stone accompanied a later burial, the remains of which had decayed.

The cairn itself was made of large round boulders. Downslope, a revetment of slabs had been built along the edge of the mound in an attempt to contain the cairn material. Numerous pieces of white quartz were found scattered in front of the revetment.

When the forecourt was excavated, traces of six fires were found, along with a broken pottery vessel. After its use, presumably as a focus for ceremonies, was over, the area in front of the entrance was covered by a layer of earth and small stones. At the end of the chamber's use, the space between the portal stones was blocked up with slabs, and a large 'closing' stone 1.8m (6ft) tall, was leaned up against the portal stones. Aubrey Burl has suggested that the closing stone originally stood in the centre of the forecourt, and was the symbol of the dead,

the spirit of the tomb. When the tomb was closed up, the stone was removed from its position, in effect 'killing' the tomb.

Additionally, the whole forecourt was covered by a series of large slabs, built in overlapping layers and inclined towards the tomb. This blocking was 1m (3ft) high. Amongst the blocking stones were various deposits of pottery and sea shells, and a jet bead, probably placed there during rituals connected with the sealing of the tomb.

The other cairn, Cairnholy II, occupies a small rocky knoll 150m (500ft) north of Cairnholy I. It is known as the tomb of Galdus, the mythical Scottish king. The cairn is smaller than its neighbour, measuring 21 by 12m (70 by 40ft). Most of the mound stones have been removed, leaving the orthostats and capstone of the chamber uncovered. There is no sign of a facade or revetment, but the chamber was divided and blocked in the same way as Cairnholy I. The chamber and antechamber had been cleared previous to excavation, and only a few pottery sherds and a couple of flint artefacts were found.

It is possible that the cairns were built in stages. The earliest structure may have been a simple chamber covered by a small cairn, with the long cairn, the outer part of the chamber and the forecourt dating to a later phase. This would explain the lack of a communicating door between the 'antechamber' and chamber.

# FIVE
# RITUAL STONES AND HENGES

An imaginative reconstruction of the stone circle of Cullerlie, Gordon. Information from the excavation report suggests that numerous bonfires of willow were lit to purify the site. The surrounding area, now drained and under cultivation, was probably swampy with a cover of rough grass and reeds.

The reconstruction shows the day-long activity of cutting willow to keep the fires going during ceremonies perhaps lasting into the night. A 'priest' carries out the rituals, while two women bring food and drink offerings to the site. The costumes are based on those from Danish mound sites.

In the third millennium BC, Scotland saw the wide-scale emergence of a new range of communal monuments – 'henges', stone circles and stone alignments. Although the dead were buried at many of these sites, the focus of these enigmatic landmarks seems to have been ritual and ceremonial, rather than funerary.

Stone circles are found throughout Scotland, the main ones in Grampian, Perth and Kinross, the South-West and the Outer Hebrides. Their appearance depends largely on the geology of an area, ranging from the granite boulder circle at Torhousekie, Wigtown (p. 175) to the tall, quarried pillars of gneiss at the Callanish circles in Lewis (p. 147).

There are also variations in fashion. Recumbent stone circles, for example, are concentrated in Grampian. These circles feature a prostrate stone flanked by two uprights, and often, as at Loanhead of Daviot (p. 170), have a ring cairn within, covering one or more burials.

Much of the detailed work on stone circles has been carried out by Alexander Thom who surveyed many sites in Britain and Brittany, publishing *Megalithic Sites in Britain* in 1967. Thom suggested that many of the circles were astronomical observatories, mathematically laid out using a measurement which he named the 'megalithic yard', corresponding to 0.829m (2.72ft).

Although many of his more detailed conclusions have been questioned, there is little doubt that some of the monuments could have been used for observing at least the more obvious astronomical events such as the lunar rising and setting points or the spring and autumn equinoxes. In communities which depended on farming and fishing, it would have been important to know, for example, when to expect particularly bad storms or high tides. The elements may have been regarded as gods, and it is not improbable that many rituals involved the sun and moon and were timed to coincide with their seasonal tracks across the sky.

Single stones, pairs of stones and alignments are also found throughout Scotland, in addition to circles. Again these may be connected with astronomy, but equally could be grave markers, territorial boundary markers or meeting points.

Some of Scotland's stone circles are found within henges, which are circular or elliptical areas with an

*Midmar Kirk recumbent stone circle in Gordon, which now stands within a graveyard laid out early this century*

external bank and internal ditch. Leading to the central area, one or more causeways cross the ditch. Henges are not found outside Britain. In Scotland, they have a mainly southern and eastern distribution, but extend as far north as Orkney.

The purpose of henges is unclear. Although many have deep surrounding ditches and banks, the fact that the bank was constructed outside the ditch, rather than inside it, would suggest that these earthworks were delineating an area of land rather than defending it. In addition, most henges are found in low-lying areas, again suggesting that defence was not a consideration.

Henge excavations seldom yield any evidence such as hut circles or posthole outlines to suggest that the sites were occupied on a permanent basis. Burials and pits containing artefact or bone 'offerings' are often found within, and in some cases the fill of the ditches suggests that certain depositions were deliberately placed rather than dumped as domestic rubbish. All these factors taken together suggest that henges had a ritual and ceremonial function.

In the absence of any written accounts of the ceremonial life of Scotland's early inhabitants, we are left with endless ways of interpreting the surviving evidence from henges and stone circles. Whatever their purpose, it was important enough to channel considerable resources into the building of these impressive monuments.

Quarrying and transporting the stone, excavating the ditches and erecting the standing stones were all labour-intensive. The estimate for the time involved in

Left *The standing stones on Lundin Links, Perth and Kinross, now standing on the golf course of the Lundin Ladies Golf Club. In local tradition they are the gravestones of Danish warriors defeated by MacBeth*

the construction of the ditch at the Ring of Brodgar (p. 144), for example, is 80,000 man-hours. Colin Renfrew has suggested that such projects were highly organised, involving considerable numbers of people, and implying the existence of centralised chiefdoms in areas such as Orkney.

Another major problem with the interpretation of stone circles and henges, as with chambered tombs, is that many of the sites went through several phases, being rebuilt or rearranged as the fashions changed. Long after their original builders had died, they were still being used as places for burial and ritual practices.

A few of Scotland's standing stones, such as at Ballymeanoch in Argyll (p. 163), bear carved designs known as cup-and-ring marks. Such carvings have also been found on cist covers, and the stonework of chambered tombs, but the most impressive examples have been cut into isolated rock out-crops found mainly in south-west Scotland and Argyll. Whether they were purely decorative, or were somehow connected to ritual is unknown.

# THE STONES OF STENNESS

Between the inland lochs of Stenness and Harray, on Orkney Mainland, are two peninsulas now connected by a road bridge, but which in the Neolithic and Bronze Age were probably joined by land.

Both promontories have complexes of standing stones. On the northern peninsula is the massive Ring of Brodgar (p. 144), while on the southern peninsula is the Stenness circle, the remains of a stone circle within a henge. Four unusually shaped stones, the tallest one over 5m (16ft) high, are all that remain of the Stenness circle. It is thought that there were originally 12 stones in the 30m (100ft) circle.

Although the stones are the most obvious feature of the site, the now ploughed-out bank and ditch of the henge would originally have been just as impressive. The ditch was 2m (6ft 6in) deep and 7m (23ft) wide, and was crossed by one entrance. Estimates suggest that quarrying the 1250 tons of solid sandstone to form the ditch could have taken up to 50,000 man-hours.

Excavations were carried out at the henge in 1973–4 by Graham Ritchie, who excavated an area in the centre of the henge as well as a section of the ditch. A post probably stood in the centre of the henge at one time. This was followed by a square setting of slabs containing, in its upper layers, cremated bone, charcoal and pottery. A couple of other stone-holes were found in the centre, and the remains of what may have been a small timber structure.

Radiocarbon dating of animal bones found in the bottom of the ditch indicated that the henge was built in the early third millennium BC. The bones were of domestic cattle, sheep and dog. The remains of the cattle and sheep were mainly mandibles and the extremities of limbs, suggesting that the carcasses had been jointed. Perhaps after ceremonies involving feasting the bones were placed in the ditch. The dating of the bones was backed up by the discovery of Neolithic grooved ware pottery.

Because of its setting, the site has drawn many visitors, and descriptions and sketches survive from the eighteenth century onwards. From these records, it seems that at the beginning of the nineteenth century four stones plus the stump of a fifth were still standing, and a further large stone was on the ground near the centre. Walter Scott visited the site in 1814 and later used it as the setting for the climax of his novel *The Pirate*.

On Christmas Day 1814 the tenant farmer, Captain W. MacKay, tried to destroy these remaining stones, angry that visitors to the site were damaging his fields. The historian Malcolm Laing, entertaining some friends in Papdale House near Kirkwall was alerted to what was going on at Stenness. One of his guests was the Sheriff Substitute of Orkney, Alexander Peterkin. He issued a suspension against MacKay until the issue was resolved.

MacKay had broken up one stone in the circle and felled another before he was stopped. His actions roused the anger of the locals and there were two attempts to set fire to his property.

The first accurate survey of the site was made in the winter of 1848, by Captain F.W.L. Thomas, Lieutenant commanding H.M. surveying vessel *Woodlark*, under less than ideal conditions:

. . . although a labour of love, it [the survey] was not accomplished without much difficulty, principally owing to the uncertain state of the weather and the distance of the locality from my residence. After a long ride, there was first to lay out the surveying poles, then shoulder my theodolite, and march from station to station through the most insuatingly melting snow that I ever remember to have felt, often being obliged to leave my instrument and run for a quarter of a mile to gain a little warmth by the exertion. It was, however, sometimes exceedingly romantic to hear the wild swans trumpeting to each other while standing under the lee of a gigantic stone, till a snow squall from the north east passed over.

Two outlying stones in the vicinity, the Watchstone and the Barnhouse Stone are probably connected with the henge. There also used to be a perforated stone, known locally as the Odin Stone, although it was completely broken up by MacKay during his bout of destruction.

Various superstitions were connected with the Odin Stone. It was said that, if a baby was passed through the hole in the stone, it would be resistant to various diseases in later life. Older people with palsy could get relief

Left *The surviving stones of the circle at Stenness. The remains of the henge bank are visible in the foreground*

from their pain by sticking their heads or limbs through the hole. Until the stone was destroyed it was the custom to leave an offering, such as food, or even a rag or pebble, at the stone when visiting.

A further use of the stone was for marriage. There are stories of couples going first to the Temple of the Moon (the Stones of Stenness) where the woman fell down on her knees and prayed for strength to carry out the vows she would make at the Odin Stone. Both then went to the Temple of the Sun (the Ring of Brodgar) where the man did the same. Couples were married by holding their right hands through the stone and swearing to be faithful to each other. To divorce, a couple could go to Stainhouse Kirk, enter by one door and leave by different doors, from then on being legally separated.

# THE RING OF BRODGAR

Near the henge-circle of Stenness lies the larger and more complete henge-circle of Brodgar. As at Stenness, the ditch around the site is cut into solid bedrock, but at Brodgar the henge is crossed by two entrances rather than one. The volume of rock excavated from the ditch was about 4,700m³ (165,700ft³). The bank, where it survives at all, is very low, and it must have been eroded or carried away over the centuries. The deep ditch may have served a similar function to the walls of a cathedral, giving a feeling of vast enclosed space.

*One of the stones of the Ring of Brodgar, looking west over the surrounding ditch and bank towards Salt Knowe*

Today 27 stones remain standing in the circle. The positions of another 13 are known, and assuming that the stones were set out with equal distances between them, there would have been 60 in the circle originally. The present sandstone slabs are 2–4.5m (6ft 6in–15ft) in height. As with most stone circles stellar and lunar observations have been postulated using surrounding scenery or neighbouring monuments as foresights.

One of the stones in the northern part of the circle (now only a stump remains) has been carved with runes and a cross. The runes translate to the name Biorn, probably a Norse visitor.

Below *Part of the circle of sandstone slabs forming the Ring of Brodgar, with the low hills and inland lochs of Orkney Mainland in the background*

# CULLERLIE

The standing stones of Cullerlie, excavated and reconstructed, stand on low land, near Leuchar Moss in Gordon. The circle is 10m (33ft) in diameter and has eight stones. Instead of being squared-off, the stones are unshaped, although most have a pointed end embedded in a pit of gravel.

Before H.E. Kilbride-Jones' excavations in 1934, the centre of the circle had been used as a stone dump. On clearing these stones, a central cairn and seven surrounding cairns were uncovered. The outer cairns were enclosed by a single ring of boulders, and the central one by a double ring of stones.

Only one of the outer cairns was undisturbed. When its cairn stones were removed, the excavators found a capstone covering a circular pit. The soil around the pit had been burnt and contained large pieces of charcoal and cremated human bone. It seems that the bodies were burnt and then the remains buried in the same spot. Evidence of burning extended over the whole area within the circle, and under the cairns, probably representing the purification of the site after the monoliths were erected.

Apart from the charcoal and cremated bones, only one potsherd and three worked flints were found.

*The standing stones of Cullerlie, looking west. Within the circle are eight cairns each edged with a ring of stones*

# CALLANISH

Men turned to stone by an enchanter, a druid temple, a megalithic calendar and a signal beacon for extra-terrestrial craft are just a few of the suggestions which have been made to explain the complex formations of standing stones at Callanish on the Isle of Lewis.

The Callanish Stones are tall slender pillars of Lewisian gneiss, set on a ridge overlooking East Loch Roag. The main formation has a central monolith 4.7 m (15ft 6in) high surrounded by an 11.25m (37ft) circle of stones which has single lines of stones radiating out from its southern, eastern and western points and a double row from the northern point. The northern 'avenue' is 82m (270ft) long with nine stones on one side

*The thin pillars of the Callanish 1 complex, looking west, with the remains of the cairn, and the central monolith within the circle*

and ten on the other. There may originally have been more. The southern line may also have been an avenue originally. The other lines have four stones each.

A layer of peat about 1.5m (5ft) thick covered the lower part of the pillars until 1857 when it was stripped for fuel by the proprietor of the island, Sir James Matheson. In the course of removing the peat, the remains of a small chambered cairn were found within the circle, in its eastern sector. Two of the stones of the circle had been incorporated into this circular cairn, and the central monolith also stood within its kerb. The entrance to the chamber faced east, and led into a 2m (6ft 6in) long passage and a small chamber divided by projecting slabs. A few tiny fragments of bone were recovered from the cairn, but nothing else.

Like most stone circles, an astronomical theory is the one most often put forward to explain Callanish's

Above *The five slabs of Ceann Hulavig (Callanish IV)
grouped around the remains of a small cairn*

Top Left *Looking north at the two concentric circles of
Cnoc Fillibhir (Callanish III). In the background is
Callanish township and East Loch Roag*

Left *Cnoc Ceann a' Gharaidh (Callanish II) looking east
at the five uprights and a fallen stone forming an elipse
around the remains of a small cairn*

existence. The degree of accuracy to which astronomical events could be predicted remains questionable. Obviously, the more stones remaining at a site, the greater the likelihood that some of them will line up with an astronomical event by coincidence. Thom thought that the east row at Callanish could have been aligned on the rising of the star Altair in 1760 BC and the north east avenue on Capella in 1790 BC, but such minute observations seem unlikely.

It is more probable that the builders of the Callanish setting and other alignments were interested in the general movements of the sun and moon, for the timing of religious events, deciding when to plant and harvest, and predicting tides.

The main setting of stones is known as Callanish I, but there are other smaller settings in the vicinity – Cnoc Ceann a' Gharaidh (Callanish II), an ellipse of seven stones (two prostrate), Cnoc Fillibhir (Callanish III), a double circle, and Ceann Hulavig (Callanish IV), five stones in an oval.

The stones have long figured in the customs of the local people. Up until last century, the people in the surrounding area would gather at the stones on midsummer morning, when is was said that 'something', probably some kind of spirit, processed down the avenue, heralded by the cuckoo's song.

# TEMPLE WOOD

Near the Nether Largie tombs (p. 130) in Argyll is a site classified as a stone circle, Temple Wood. An almost perfect circle of stones 12m (40ft) in diameter was the focus for centuries of burials. The circle is displayed in its final form, almost covered by a cairn of stones. The site is 250m (820ft) from Nether Largie South Cairn to the north-east and 300m (1000ft) from the Nether Largie standing stones (p. 166) to the south-east.

The site has been excavated twice, first in 1929 by J.H. Craw and secondly in 1974–9 by J.G. Scott.

Through the excavations, the sequence of structures on the site has been established. A circle of 22 stones was the earliest construction. Not all had been left standing – some were only known from their postholes. Two of the stones were decorated, one with concentric circles, the other with a double spiral, half of it on one face, the other half on the adjoining face. Possible cupmarks were found on one of the other stones.

Various burials were made in and around the circle, although it is difficult to know exactly when in the sequence this occurred. Two cairns were constructed outside the stone circle, one on the north-east, the other on the west. Beneath them were cists containing inhumation burials. The west cairn was surrounded by upright stones with drystone walling between, and a

*Temple Wood stone circle, and encircling cairn, looking from the site of an adjacent stone circle*

*Temple Wood stone circle in its final phase, surrounded by a large cairn. In the centre is the remains of a cist with the kerbstones of its original cairn*

large slab covered its cist. When it was raised, the cist was found to have been paved with flat stones. On the paving was a layer of earth and the tooth of a 4–6 year-old child. The phosphate content of the soil indicated an inhumation.

The cist of the north-east cairn was covered by an even larger slab. This time the floor of the cist was of

pebbles, on which lay a beaker, a flint scraper and three barbed and tanged arrowheads. Again analysis of the soil indicated an inhumation burial.

Burials were also found inside the circle. In the centre was a cist burial, again covered by a cairn surrounded by a kerb. The slabs forming the cist were set in a pit with part of them above ground. The capstone was missing, suggesting that the cist had been opened previously. A few fragments of cremated bone were found in the cist.

At some point smaller orthostats were erected between the freestanding monoliths of the monument, forming a closed circle. A cairn of stones was built up around the circle, covering the external cairns.

It is recorded that around the end of the eighteenth century a hoard of coins, presumably medieval, was found near the centre of the circle. The trees around the site were planted in the late nineteenth century and the site was given the name Temple Wood.

In 1979 a further circle was discovered to the north of Temple Wood. Concrete markers now reconstruct its major phases – an earlier timber setting later replaced by upright stones. The posts had been removed but from the holes it seems there were at least six and possibly nine in the circle, with an additional one in the centre. The later stone circle had at least five stones, again with one in the centre.

# BALBIRNIE

The stone circle of Balbirnie, Kirkcaldy District was excavated by Graham Ritchie in 1970–1 prior to road-widening, and was later re-erected 125m (400ft) from its original position.

The first structure on the site was a setting of ten standing stones, some dolerite, others sandstone. When the site was excavated, only five stones were visible, and the stumps of three others were found. The other two had been removed when a nearby wall was built. Cremated bone was found in five of the stone sockets, presumably a sacrificial offering made as the site was erected. Grooved ware pottery was found in one of the sockets. At the centre of the circle and set into the ground was a square setting of stones.

A series of four cists was dug into the ground inside the circle. One was full of soil mixed with small fragments of cremated bone and charcoal; another contained the cremations of an adult female and a child. A third also had the cremations of an adult female and a child, in addition to a food vessel and a flint knife. One of the stones in this cist was decorated with 17 cup marks. The final cist only had one stone surviving, and a jet button was all it contained. A beaker and a jet bead were found in a separate deposit.

All four of these cists had been covered with a cairn of small boulders which completely filled the centre of the circle. The remains of at least 16 cremated bodies had been inserted into the cairn or scattered over it at a later stage.

*The reconstruction of Balbirnie stone circle, showing some of the standing stones, the central paved area, and one of the cists*

Balbirnie, and the nearby henge site of Balfarg (p. 177) may have formed a ceremonial centre for the surrounding area from about 3000 BC for over a millennium. Although burials were recorded at both sites, the primary function of the sites may not have been funerary. They were probably the locations of ceremonies and rituals, and perhaps even political meetings.

# TWELVE APOSTLES

In a low-lying area of land between the Cluden Water and the River Nith in Nithsdale, lies the largest stone circle on mainland Scotland, and the fifth largest in Britain. It is a flattened circle 88m (290ft) in diameter, now split by a hedge and close to the road, but still impressive. It has been called both the 'Twelve Apostles' and the 'Druidical Circle'. The nearby village of Holywood got its name from a grove of oaks which surrounded the circle.

Four of the stones are boulders, probably obtained locally, but the others were quarried, perhaps from a source 12km ($7\frac{1}{2}$ miles) distant. The circle is most similar to the Cumbrian stone circles.

The earliest plan of the site appeared in Grose's *Antiquities of Scotland*, and was drawn in 1789. It shows twelve boulders. By 1844, the New Statistical Account recorded eleven boulders. The explanation for the disappearance of a stone usually involved Judas Iscariot's treachery.

When Fred Coles studied the site in the 1890s, he was surprised to find that on the 25-inch map the twelfth stone had mysteriously reappeared. He got in touch with H.M. Survey who cleared the mystery up – the twelfth stone was an accidental blue spot reproduced by zincography on the published plans.

*The Twelve Apostles from the south-east with some stones obscured by the barley crop. A hedge now splits the circle*

# MACHRIE MOOR

On moorland near the disused Moss Farm on Arran are a remarkable number of prehistoric sites, mainly Neolithic and Bronze Age. In addition to hut circles, field systems, chambered cairns and round cairns, there are at least six stone circles, all in close proximity.

Many of the sites have been excavated or investigated. One day in May 1861, J. Bryce dug into three of the circles, and then opened five more sites on a September day in the same year.

Only five circles were exposed before Aubrey Burl's excavations in 1978 which uncovered the stones of another circle almost totally hidden by peat formation. Ten stones were uncovered, with evidence for an earlier ring of timber posts between them.

The most spectacular site on Machrie Moor has three of its sandstone uprights remaining, standing up to 5.5m (18ft) high. Originally there were a further four or five stones in the circle, and remains of these lie around the monoliths, including an abandoned attempt at turning one of the pillars into a pair of millstones.

When Bryce dug into the site in 1861, two cists were found under a thick layer of peat. One cist contained four flakes of flint and a food vessel with bands of decoration covering its surface. The other cist contained no artefacts or bones. Bryce thought it had not been used, but it is possible that any human remains had decayed.

The other monolith remaining on Machrie Moor belonged to a circle of at least six stones. The pillar is over 4m (13ft) high, its top patterned by gradual

---

*Below* The ring of four boulders on Machrie Moor, with the monoliths of two other circles in the background

*Right* The one remaining erect monolith from a circle of at least six stones on Machrie Moor

*The three weathered monoliths of the most spectacular of*
*the Machrie Moor sites*

weathering processes. In the centre of this circle Bryce
found a capstone, 'held down' with eight stones. In the
cist were some flint flakes and an urn which disinte-
grated on handling, but no human remains. A second
cist to the south contained a crouched inhumation
burial, accompanied by two flint flakes, but no vessel.

The tall pillars of these two circles are of red
sandstone. Each pillar was estimated to weigh between
eight and ten tons. Similar sandstone can be found in the
bed of the Machrie Water 1km ($\frac{1}{2}$ mile) away, but Bryce
thought the stones were more likely to have been
quarried from the shore, 3km (2 miles) away.

The remaining circles are all formed of boulders. The
smallest setting is a ring of four. It is not known if there
were originally more stones in the setting. A cist had

been placed in the centre of this setting. There was a
fragmented urn in one corner, decorated only on its
upper part. Under the fragments were some bone
fragments and on the cist floor were three flint flakes
and a bronze pin.

Another of the boulder settings was formed of two
concentric circles of rounded granite boulders. The
inner one was a true circle of eight boulders, while the
outer contained 14 boulders and was elliptical. It is not
clear whether these circles were both free standing or if
the outer circle formed the kerb of a platform on which
the inner circle was set. There was a cist in the centre but
it had been opened before Bryce investigated it. This
setting is known locally as Fingal's Cauldron Seat. One
of the stones has a perforation where it is said, Fingal
tied his hound Bran while he attended to cooking
matters beside the cauldron stand.

The final circle was of 12 stones, although several are

*The concentric boulder rings of 'Fingal's Cauldron Seat', on Machrie Moor*

missing. It is formed of granite boulders alternating with sandstone slabs. Recent excavations uncovered a cremation near the circle's centre. It was under an inverted cordoned urn, and was accompanied by a bone needle and a flint knife.

It is possible that the circles and cists on Machrie Moor are not strictly contemporary. The cists may have been inserted into the centre of the circles after their erection and use.

The area must have been the ritual focus for the surrounding communities. It is possible that each circle was dedicated to a different god, and offerings would be made, and help sought, at different circles according to the nature of the problem, perhaps in a similar way that chapels are dedicated to different saints within a cathedral.

# ACHAVANICH

Near Loch Stemster in Caithness is an unusual horse-shoe-shaped arrangement of small standing stones. The tallest stone is only 2m (6ft 6in) high. Some stones may have been taller, but weathering has caused them to crack and split. Only 36 stones remain in the setting, although there may have been about 54 originally. At most stone circles the flat faces of the stones follow the line of the setting, but at Achavanich the flat faces are 'side on'. The stone slabs appear to have been set into a low mound of earth and stone, possibly the result of levelling the central area.

Only one other site of this type survives, at Broubster, also in Caithness, although similar open-ended settings of stone, earth and wood have been recognised along the east coast of Britain. Another horseshoe setting, laid out within two parallel rows of stones, is thought to have existed at Latheronwheel, on the coast 8km (5 miles) south of Achavanich, but it was broken up during drystone wall building in the late nineteenth century. The purpose and date of these settings are unknown, but they are usually assumed to belong to the Bronze Age.

Outside the north-east corner of the setting at Achavanich, some small slabs, possibly the remains of cist burials, protrude through the turf. Close to the south-east of the setting is a round, heather-covered cairn, situated on a knoll. The faint outlines remaining suggest it was about 18m (60ft) in diameter. Some stones from the chamber can be seen sticking through

*Achavanich stone setting, Caithness, looking north-east from the open end of the horseshoe, and showing the mound into which the stones are set*

the rubble near the heart of the mound. The tallest stone formed the back of the chamber.

The chambered cairn would have been Neolithic, probably earlier than the stone setting. The fact that the setting and the later cist burials were built in the same area as the chambered cairn shows that the region remained one of ritual importance over the centuries.

Right *Looking from the chambered cairn at Achavanich towards the horseshoe setting beside the roadside. In the foreground is one of the stones of the chamber*

# MID CLYTH

The Mid Clyth stone rows, Caithness, otherwise known as the Hill o'Many Stanes, are an impressive arrangement of at least 22 rows of small flat stones (less than 1m (3ft 3in) high) running north to south across the hilltop. Today there are around 200 stones, but if the pattern is 'completed' it suggests that there may originally have been over 600 stones. The stones form a fan-shape, spreading out down the hillside.

As no stone rows have been excavated in Scotland, their purpose is uncertain. G.E. Hutchinson has suggested that the stones are 'the ruins of mathematical instruments of some sort'. Thom calculated that by looking south along the most easterly row, it would have been possible to see the winter maximum moonrise, and that by looking north along the most westerly row, the summer maximum moonrise could have been observed.

In local tradition, the stones mark the site of a battle between two rival clans, the Keiths and the Gunns. The Keiths were about to win the day when one of the Gunns lying wounded on the ground gave the leader of the Keiths a blow which divided the main tendon of one of his legs. The Keiths retreated and the Gunns set up a memorial to the day by burying the dead of both clans in rows, marking the head of each dead warrior with a stone.

*Mid Clyth Stone Rows, the Hill o'Many Stanes, looking southwards down the hill with some displaced stones in the foreground*

# BEACHARRA

Known locally as 'Leac-an-Fhamhair' (the flagstone of the giant), the standing stone at Beacharra is almost 5m (16ft) in height, the tallest in Kintyre.

Excavation of single standing stones such as that at Beacharra often does not tell much more than the proportion of the stone underground, the shape of the socket and whether there was packing material around its base. Occasionally stone cairns are found at the base, with a grave beneath. Scraps of bone or pottery may be found in the socket, possibly an offering if the stone was dedicated.

Many suggestions have been made as to the purpose of single standing stones. An astronomical purpose is often suggested, marking either an observation point, or a foresight.

The stones may have been simply grave markers, perhaps marking the burial place of a respected member of a group such as its healer or leader.

Alternatively, they could have been territorial markers erected by groups staking out the extent of their lands, or meeting places or rallying points for members of a scattered community.

*Beacharra Standing Stone, the tallest in Kintyre. It was connected with fertility rites until relatively recently*

# BALLYMEANOCH

The standing stones at Ballymeanoch are part of the large concentration of monuments in the Kilmartin area of Argyll. The stones are arranged in two linear settings, almost parallel, with four stones in one setting, and two in the other. Near the two-stone setting is a fallen stone with a hole pierced through it.

The two middle stones of the four-stone setting are decorated with cup and cup-and-ring marks, and there is one cup on the southern stone. Thom believed that this alignment was for observation of the declination of the sun at the winter solstice.

Thom thought the stone alignment was also connected with the moon rising in its most southerly position, but could offer no suggestion as to what the foresight may have been, due to the view being blocked by trees.

From sketches, the holed stone has fallen within the last hundred years. The area around it was recently excavated. Some deposits of cremated bone were found in the socket hole. The local explanation for the holed stone was similar to that for the Odin Stone at Stenness in Orkney (p. 141), namely that it was used for hand holding to seal contracts, including marriage, but in this case the hole is too small to allow this.

*The four-stone alignment at Ballymeanoch, looking north*

Left *The Ballymeanoch alignments, looking south*

# KINTRAW

Overlooking Loch Craignish, Argyll and the surrounding hills and islands is the site of Kintraw. It has often been cited by archaeoastronomers as demonstrating that its designers were interested in accurate astronomical observation rather than general seasonal change.

The site comprises a large cairn, a smaller one and a standing stone. The cairns were excavated in 1959–60. Surrounding the larger cairn was a kerb, inside which was a small slab-built cist covered by a capstone. The cist had been divided in two using a further slab and some fragments of cremated bone were found in one of the compartments. Shells, animal teeth and six jet beads lay on the old land surface and among the cairnstones, but these could have been dropped at a later date and filtered through. Around the perimeter of the cairn was a large amount of quartz and some rock crystals which may originally have covered the surface of the mound to give it a glittery appearance.

The smaller cairn had a kerb of large boulders, with a small cist built up against its inside. All that was found were a few fragments of carbonised wood.

The standing stone collapsed in the spring of 1979 and the socket was excavated before the stone was re-erected in a bed of concrete. Little was gleaned apart from the fact that the socket had been packed with stones to help support the monolith.

*Kintraw Standing Stone, Argyll. In the foreground is the edge of the larger cairn, and just beyond the stone, the outline of the smaller cairn*

Thom and others have believed the site could have been used to mark the sunset at the mid-winter solstice, by sighting onto a notch in the Paps of Jura between Ben Shiantaidh and Ben a'Chaolais, 43km (27 miles) away on the horizon. The notch cannot be seen from the site itself, being obscured by some land jutting into Loch Craignish, so the sun's movements relative to the notch would have had to have been observed from higher ground, perhaps a terrace or platform on the nearby hillside.

Along the sight line from this platform to the distant notch a post would have been positioned, and the cairn built round it. (Evidence that a pole had stood in the cairn was found during excavation.) Once the cairn was built, it would have given the observer enough height to view the notch. In the following years, an observer standing on the cairn would, theoretically, have known it was the solstice when the sun was seen to rise through the notch. It is suggested that the monolith was used in different observations, perhaps in conjunction with the smaller cairn.

A major problem with using such a distant site as the Paps of Jura would have been a lack of clarity due to the mist and rain characteristic of coastal west Scotland.

*The view of the Kintraw stone and cairn from the platform on the hillside, showing the 'notch' in the Paps of Jura in the background*

# NETHER LARGIE

In fields about 250m (820ft) from the Temple Wood stone circles (p. 150) is a complex of various settings of standing stones in a line running north-east to south-west.

At both the south end and the north end of the alignment is a pair of standing stones, around 2.8m (9ft 2in) high. In both pairs, one face of one stone has three cup marks carved on it.

Twenty-four metres north-east of the southern pair of stones is a group of four stones, all less than 1m (3ft 3in) high, although they may have been damaged. One of them is lying on the ground.

Close to these stones is a group of five stones in a cross formation, only three of which are still in position. The stone central to the cross has 40 cup marks, and three cups with rings at least partially surrounding them. It is a large stone, 2.8m (9ft 2in) high, whereas the others are smaller.

Thom believed that by lining up one arm of the cross with the circle at Temple Wood and siting onto the peak of Bellanock Hill, the moon's minimum positions every 18.61 years could be observed, and that the various stones in the alignment indicated critical positions for an observer of the lunar maxima.

*The cup-marked stone which forms the central monolith in the cross-shaped setting at Nether Largie, Argyll*

# ORWELL

On a low hillock at the north end of Loch Leven, in arable land, are two standing stones 2.8m (9ft 2in) and 3.8m (12ft 6in) in height. One is slightly rounded, the other more rugged.

Some cists and burials were found near the stones in the nineteenth century, during ploughing. The stones seem to have marked an area for burial, and perhaps ritual gatherings, during the Bronze Age.

The smaller western stone fell over in the early 1970s and the area around each stone was excavated before the fallen stone was re-erected. The fallen stone had been set in a hollow, near which was discovered a deposit of cremated bone. The other stone was set in a proper socket. Two cremation deposits were found within the socket, and must have been placed there just as the stone was being erected. The cremations were placed one above the other, with a horizontal slab separating them. The deposits represented the cremations of several people, and, in addition, the excavators found bones of dog and pig.

*The rounded and angular pillars of Orwell standing stones, looking north-west*

# BALLOCHROY

At Ballochroy on the Kintyre coast is a group of three standing stones arranged in a line.

There was a large stone cairn at the south-east end of the alignment at one time, but most of it has been removed, and all that remains is a scatter of stones and the stone cist which would have been at the heart of the cairn.

The astronomical explanation is that the setting of stones was for observation of the midsummer setting sun behind Ben Cara in Jura.

Right *The standing stones and remains of the cist at Ballochroy, Argyll*

Below *Sunset over the Ballochroy Standing Stones, with the Paps of Jura in the background*

# STRONTOILLER

At the mouth of Glen Lonan in Lorn, Argyll, is a group of three sites – a standing stone, a stone circle and a cairn. The standing stone is by far the most impressive of the three. It stands 4m (13ft) high, a rough-cut, lichen covered monolith. Along with the adjacent cairn, it is said to be the grave of Diarmid, the Irish hero.

Before excavation in 1967 by Graham Ritchie, the cairn looked like a setting of granite boulders. It had already been opened to get to the burial. All that was found in the central area was a small scatter of cremated

bone, and various patches of burning, perhaps the remains of a funeral pyre. Alternatively, the burning could have been due to scrub clearance prior to building the cairn. Around the bases of the boulders forming the kerb of the cairn, quartz chips and pebbles had been scattered – quartz is often found in association with Bronze Age burials in Argyll.

The stone circle lies to the north of the standing stone and cairn. Its 31 stones are not large; they are rounded boulders of varying sizes, none more than 1m (3ft 3in) in height. The interior of the circle has no features to suggest a central cairn.

*The Standing Stone at Strontoiller, Lorn, Argyll. In the background is the outline of the cairn*

# LOANHEAD OF DAVIOT

One of the best-known recumbent stone circles is Loanhead of Daviot, in Gordon. It is situated near the summit of a conspicuous hill, on a level 'shelf'.

The circle is 20.5m (67ft) in diameter, and consists of eight standing stones, plus the recumbent and two flanking stones. The stone beside the east flanker has a vertical line of at least five cupmarks on its inner face.

At one time it was thought that the recumbent was a 'double' recumbent, but it was later found to be one stone, split by the elements. In front of the recumbent was a space delineated by a kerb of stones, possibly a ritual area.

When the site was excavated in 1935 by H.E. Kilbride-Jones, each stone was found to be surrounded by a small cairn. Charcoal and pottery had been placed in pits beneath these cairns. In the middle of the circle was a pit covered by a large kerbed ring cairn which took up most of the central area. Four shallow pits may be the remains of postholes for some kind of temporary mortuary structure. The cairn had been built over a burnt area containing pottery, flint and cremated bones.

Beside the circle is another circular area, enclosed by two arcs of low stone walling. This site was excavated in 1935 and was found to be an enclosed Bronze Age cremation cemetery. The excavations uncovered a burial in a shallow central pit – the incomplete cremation of a 40 year-old man. Subsequent cremations had been made on the same spot. More burials have been found in the area around the circle, in urns or pits.

*The enclosed cremation cemetery at Loanhead of Daviot, with the recumbent stone circle in the background*

Right *Loanhead of Daviot recumbent stone circle, showing the recumbent and flankers, the central cairn, and two of the monoliths in the circle.*

# SUNHONEY

The recumbent stone circle of Sunhoney near Echt in Gordon stands on the shoulder of a hill, surrounded by a ring of aging trees – oak, ash, pine, maple, and beech.

There are nine stones in the circle, plus the recumbent and its two flankers. The recumbent has fallen over and part of it has broken off. In the centre of the circle is the outline of a ring cairn, which was investigated in 1865 by Charles Elphinstone Dalrymple. Some cremated bones and traces of burning were found.

On what is now the top of the recumbent, but what would have been its outer face, are 31 cup marks. They are plain cups, without encircling rings. Although it has been claimed in the past that they were natural, numerous examinations by geologists and archaeologists have confirmed that they are man-made.

The cup marks found on standing stones and on rock outcrops are similar. They could have been made by rotating a round stone or pebble. Most of them are simple cups, but occasionally pairs are joined together by a line. Usually the patterning is random although in some cases, as at Loanhead of Daviot (p. 170), the cup marks are arranged in lines. Even if the patterning is random, the area in which the cupmarks are carved, at least in recumbent stone circles, seems to be well defined. Cups are restricted to the recumbent, the flankers, or the stone adjacent to one of the flankers.

Of all the folklore linked with the Aberdeenshire stone circles, there is none which provides an adequate explanation for the cup marks. One theory is that the cups were to hold blood from sacrifices made on the recumbent stone 'altar'. This is improbable – at Sunhoney, for example, the cups were carved in the vertical face of the recumbent stone.

There have been a number of other suggestions. The cups are sometimes seen as plans of circular huts, perhaps representing the settlements in the surrounding area. Another suggestion is that they are mason's marks made by those erecting the stones of a circle. The supposed connection of many stones and circles with astronomy has led to the suggestion that the cups are planetary charts, but none match up with even the most prominent constellations. A further theory is that they were an early form of writing, but they do not seem to conform to groups divisible into an alphabet.

From their position on the stones, an astronomical link seems most likely. It is thought that they were placed at the point in the circle over which the moon rose or set at the major standstill. At Sunhoney, the moonrise is first visible over the decorated recumbent.

*The cup-mark decorated recumbent stone and flankers of the Sunhoney circle*

# EASTER AQUHORTHIES

Situated on the side of a hill near Inverurie in Gordon is the recumbent stone circle of Easter Aquhorthies.

The circle, 19.5m (64ft) in diameter, comprises nine stones set in a low bank, a huge 3.8m (12ft 6in) recumbent and two flankers. In addition, in front of the recumbent are two huge blocks of stone delineating an area, perhaps for ceremonial purposes.

At Easter Aquhorthies, the circle's designers used geology to heighten the differences in shape and size between the recumbent and flankers and the other

stones. The stones in the circle are all of pink porphyry apart from the one next to the east flanker which is of red jasper. These stones are graded in height decreasing from the 2.25m (7ft 4in) flankers to the stones opposite the recumbent which are 1.7m (5ft 7in) high.

The flankers are grey granite, and the recumbent is red granite which has come from near Bennachie. Some of the stones have been shaped, for example, the recumbent's outer face has been worked smooth.

As the site has not been excavated, it is not known whether there is a central ring cairn or not, but an early reference to a cist, and the rise in the profile of the interior, suggests that there may have been.

*The recumbent stone circle of Easter Aquhorthies, looking at the southern half of the circle with the massive recumbent, and flankers*

# TORHOUSEKIE

At Torhousekie in the Bladnoch Valley, Wigtown, is a stone circle unlike others in the south-west of Scotland. It is most similar to the recumbent stone circles around Kincardine, where the recumbent stone is within the circle rather than in the circumference.

The 19 granite boulders which make up the circle are set on a slightly raised platform of small stones and earth. It is probable that they are from a local source, though none is obvious. The largest boulder in the circle weighs six tons, and is situated in the south-east

sector, with the other stones graded in size and the smallest stones opposite the largest. The boulders do not seem to have been shaped in any way. The south-east sector is further distinguished by being 'flattened' in outline.

In the centre of the circle, and in front of the largest boulders, is a line of three stones, two larger ones, with a smaller one between. This was known locally in the seventeenth century as 'King Galdus' tomb'. These three stones are at the straight side of a D-shaped outline of stones and earth, probably a ring cairn.

It is thought that the Torhousekie circle provides a link between the recumbent stone circles of the north-east of Scotland and another group in the south-west of Ireland.

*The stone circle at Torhousekie in the Bladnoch Valley, with its central arrangement of a small boulder flanked by two larger ones*

# BROOMEND OF CRICHIE

A small henge is all that remains of a complex of late Neolithic sites in the area around the confluence of the rivers Don and Urie. An avenue of stones once led north from the henge to a large setting of stones – three concentric rings with a cairn in the centre. This setting has since been destroyed by quarrying.

The henge was excavated by Charles Elphinstone Dalrymple in 1855. A wide ditch enclosing a small central area was crossed by two entranceways more or less aligned with the avenue.

Originally there were six stones within the henge. Only two remain – the third is a Pictish symbol stone which was moved there for safe keeping last century. Burial deposits in pits and vessels had been made at the base of each stone. In front of one stone, for example, was a circular stone-lined pit containing cremated bones. Nearby was a decorated sandstone battle axe and an inverted cordoned urn with more cremated bones inside. In the middle of the setting was a cist containing a skeleton and some cremated bones.

The avenue, which may have had 36 stones (only three remain), continued south from the henge. Four cists, two containing oxhide-covered double burials with beakers, were found in a sandbank near its southern end.

*Broomend of Crichie henge, looking south from the north entrance. The middle stone is Pictish. In the background is one of the three remaining stones of the avenue*

# BALFARG

The site of Balfarg henge occupies an open area, now within a housing estate, in the town of Glenrothes, Fife. The henge was recognised from an aerial photograph and excavated before the estate was built. After the excavations, the estate was replanned, allowing the site to be preserved.

The site, 60m (200ft) in diameter, is delineated by a circular ditch 2.5m (8ft) deep, with an external bank. One narrow causeway provided access across the ditch. Excavation, by Roger Mercer in the late 1970s, revealed, in the central area, a circular setting of 16 pits, which had contained posts. Sherds of grooved ware pottery were found in the packing of the postholes. Samples from the timber ring gave a date of around 3000 BC for the early phase of the site.

Short posts now mark the position of the original timber posts which were probably much taller. In addition to the main timber ring there were concentric outlines of smaller, closely spaced rings of timber, which may have been fenced areas.

Some time after the timber circles had been erected, two stone circles were put up, an inner one of five stones (one remains) and an outer one detected from an arc of hollows in the north-east. The stone beside the entrance probably belongs to this phase of construction. If the spacing between these stones was constant, the outer circle had 24 stones and the inner one twelve. The two stones remaining are dolerite slabs, possibly from the Lomond Hills.

*Looking across the excavated ditch of Balfarg henge. The posts mark the position of the timber circle and the figure that of the grave*

In the interior of the henge was a two-ton slab covering an oval pit full of dark soil. From the position of some teeth and a small part of a left tibia, the excavator was able to determine that the pit had contained the crouched inhumation of a young adult, buried on the right side. Close to where the hands would have been was a handled beaker, its mouth covered with a thin slab, and a small knife of black flint was found nearby. Given the date of the site, this burial was probably made at a late stage in the henge's use.

# CAIRNPAPPLE HILL

From the summit of Cairnpapple Hill in West Lothian, if the day is clear, you can see the Bass Rock in the North Sea to the east, the Pentland and Moorfoot Hills of the Borders to the south, the Ochill Hills to the north, and away to the west, the mountains of Arran in the Firth of Clyde. It is an exposed vantage point, but the panorama is spectacular.

The hilltop was chosen as a 'ritual' and burial site around 2800 BC, and was used by succeeding groups of people until about 1500 BC. It would have been an ideal spot from which to observe the rising and setting of the sun and moon in all seasons.

The site in its final form, a large burial cairn surrounded by a ditch and bank, gave the hill its name. It is thought that Kernepopple, the name in use by the early seventeenth century, comes from the Gaelic 'carn' (cairn) and the Old English 'popel' (a heap of loose stones).

As would be expected of a site which was in use for over 1000 years, its layout and focal point changed to accommodate the ideas of successive groups. The sequence was unravelled by Stuart Piggott who excavated the site in the 1940s.

For the late Neolithic community who first used the site, clearing the summit of the hill of its covering of oak

*The main beaker grave of the second phase at Cairnpapple Hill, which is now housed within a concrete shell representing the extent of the solid cairn of the first Bronze Age cairn*

and hazel scrub was the primary task. This done, seven holes were dug in the rock, arranged in an arc. A handful of cremated human bone was placed in each of six of the holes, and five other deposits of cremated bone were dug into the old ground surface. Two of the cremations had bone pins with them, of a type which have been found in many late Neolithic cremation cemeteries in England. In the centre of the arc were three sockets which, from their shape and size, probably held standing stones.

Fragments of two stone axes were found in the early levels of the site. They were examined petrologically to see if their origin could be determined. The samples matched up exactly with material from two stone axe 'factories' – Langdale in the Lake District and Penmaenmawr Mountain in North Wales. This is important as it suggests that as well as using locally available products, the communities using Cairnpapple were engaged in some form of trade with more distant groups.

In the next period of its use, the site was remodelled as a henge. Twenty-four standing stones were erected in an oval, surrounded by a ditch with a bank to the outside, enclosing an area about 60m (200ft) in diameter. The ditch was crossed by two entrances, one at the north, the other at the south. Inside were various pits and hearths but few finds – only fragments of cremated bone and some pieces of beaker pottery.

There were also two graves within the area of the henge. One grave was rectangular, cut into the rock, and contained fragments of a beaker in one corner. Unfortunately, in this grave, as in the other, the acid soil had destroyed any bones. The second grave was marked with a standing stone and had a setting of stones round the grave. The body had been accompanied by two beakers and two wooden objects.

The next activity on the site involved the construction of a massive burial cairn within the henge. It seems likely that the stone circle was dismantled to provide material for the cairn – 21 stones up to almost 2.7m (9ft) in length formed part of the kerb. The dimensions of these stones match up with the dimensions of the holes in the circle. The cairn covered two Bronze Age cist-burials, the central one an inhumation with a food vessel, the other a cremation. The cairn also covered the beaker burial of the previous phase.

At a later date, the diameter of the cairn was doubled and a new kerb of 60 rounded boulders built. Within the enlarged area were two cremations covered with inverted cinerary urns, dating to the later Bronze Age.

The final burials at the site were in four graves dug within the ditched area. The bones had decayed and there were no artefacts to provide clues to their age, but they are probably Iron Age.

# BALUACHRAIG

At Baluachraig in the Kilmartin Valley, is a cup-and-ring marked outcrop, typical of a type of site found in many parts of Scotland, most notably in Galloway and Argyll.

It is covered with over 130 plain cups and 32 cup marks with either one or two rings surrounding them. As with most other sites the rock face does not seem to have been levelled or smoothed in any way before the symbols were carved.

Because of their nature, and the fact that they are not associated with ceremony or burial, it is difficult to date these sites, but from similar carvings found in tombs and on stone circles, they are usually assigned to the late Neolithic and Bronze Age, although some symbols may have been added by later visitors to the site who wished to try their hand at carving.

The lack of certainty surrounding the date and purpose of the sites has left much scope for speculation. Many theories have been proposed – some reasonable, some improbable, some verging on the absurd.

Ronald Morris in his book *The Prehistoric Rock Art of Galloway and the Isle of Man* listed over a hundred theories concerning cup-and-ring marks.

A popular explanation is that the sites were connected with ritual. One suggestion is that the cups were used as holders for sacred food and wine, during ceremonies dedicated to a god or goddess. As to which god or goddess, contenders include an eye goddess, a mother goddess (the cup-and-rings representing breasts) and a water god (the cup-and-rings representing the ripples from a stone thrown into a pool). One theory even links the markings with the worship of cows, the symbols being stylised representations of cow pats.

An astronomical connection is another common theory. It has been suggested that prehistoric astronomers used the rocks for storing information on celestial alignments. For example, if the moon's 18.61 year cycle was being observed, there would have had to be ways of storing information year by year.

Others have claimed that they are more than merely freehand circles. Thom – after some very complex calculations – concluded that the rings were carefully measured out, using Pythagorean triangles and a measurement of 2.1cm (0.816in), his so-called 'megalithic inch'.

Others have gone to the opposite extreme, claiming that the carvings are a natural phenomenon. Some opt for decoration for its own sake as an explanation. Could they represent patterns found more commonly on the skins of the inhabitants? If so, maybe the rocks were 'tattooists' shop windows' where a prospective customer could choose a design.

Messages from outer space, gaming tables, field ploughing plans, casts for making bronze decorations – the list is seemingly endless.

Left *Baluachraig cup-and-rings, Kilmartin Valley, Argyll*

# HIGH BANKS

One of the most impressive of the south-west Scotland cup-and-ring sites is at High Banks near Kirkcudbright. Here the designs are carved on an outcrop of greywacke.

It has been recorded that there used to be many more carved outcrops in the area, but that they were destroyed in the 1830s during quarrying for rock to build the surrounding stone dykes. G. Hamilton who first noted the High Banks site searched the walls of the area for any traces of markings, but could only find one, on the copestone of a nearby bridge.

The outcrop is heavily patterned in some areas. At the south end are at least 350 cups, some close together and forming their own patterns, and many cup-and-ring marks, including some with up to four rings.

R.W.B. Morris, who has done a great deal of research into the Galloway stones, has noted that the outcrops chosen for decoration could usually be seen from a distance. In addition, the sun often shone on them for most of the day.

Morris thought that there may be some connection between the distribution of cup-and-ring marked rocks and the areas where copper and gold are found. He notes that the districts where copper has been worked and rivers panned coincide very closely with the stones, all but two of the cup-and-ring sites being within 12.5km (7¾ miles) of known copper workings.

A similar situation has been noted by Morris for the Argyll sites. He suggested that the sites were connected with 'copper-searching magic' but felt that some of the sites were too distant from copper sources to justify the time and energy needed to decorate them so richly. He thought it possible that these more distant outcrops were training schools for apprentice priests and prospectors being taught the symbols which they would need to carry out their task.

Just how the marks were carved is another question that has intrigued researchers. Sir J.Y. Simpson (pioneer of the use of chloroform in anesthesia), who did much of the early work on recording and interpreting the cup and ring marks, noted that even where harder rocks were being carved, a flint 'celt' and wooden mallet would have been adequate. He wrote:

> In the Edinburgh Antiquarian Museum there is a block of Aberdeen granite from Kintore, forming one of the sculptured stones of Scotland, and containing upon one side two crescents, etc. . . . . On the back of this hard granite, Mr. Robert Paul, the doorkeeper of the Museum tried for me the experiment I allude to, and cut, in two hours, two thirds of circle with a flint and wooden mallet.

*High Banks cup-and-ring markings — one of the most heavily decorated areas of the outcrop*

# NEWBIGGING

Lying by a hedge on the farm of Newbigging, Perth and Kinross, is a cup-and-ring marked stone. The stone once stood upright in a nearby field, but was moved to its present position in 1981 when it was found to be listing at a 45° angle. A small excavation was carried out around it, and the monolith was found to be sitting in a bed of stones of a much more recent date than the monolith.

Documentation would bear this out. The stone was probably recumbent originally, which would be more in keeping with the way it is decorated. It may have been re-erected on more than one occasion, finally in

1894. When Fred R. Coles was recording the stones of Perthshire, he spoke to Mr McGregor the tenant farmer, and reported:

> He told me that it had been proposed to blast and remove the stone. To this Mr. McGregor strongly objected and, in lieu of consenting to this act of barbarism, he had the stone lifted and set up vertically as it now stands.

One face of the stone is covered with over fifty cup marks, some plain, others with one or more rings. Their decoration is unusual in that many of these designs are 'joined' to a main channel, giving the impression of an overall pattern rather than a number of separate entities.

*The Newbigging cup-and-ring marked stone in its new recumbent position*

# ORMAIG

At Ormaig in Argyll, is a group of six rock outcrops, decorated with cup-and-ring markings. Four of the sites have only a few markings, but two sites are richly decorated.

The lower of the two main outcrops is a sloping rock face. Part of it has been weathered, but the other area was only de-turfed in 1974. There are numerous cups, many of them plain, some with rings. There are three examples of 'rosettes', complex designs made up of a central cup and ring surrounded by a circle of small cups with a final ring surrounding them. The second of the main outcrops has some designs similar to the rosettes. These rosettes reinforce a point often made about the cup-and-ring decorated stones – although there is considerable uniformity, there was still room for innovative designs.

Ormaig has the distinction of being one of the very few cup-and-ring sites to have had any objects associated with it. During excavation of the site, a small flint tool and a tiny slate disc were found as the turf was removed. It is of course not certain if these objects were used in the carving of the rock face or dropped at a later time by visitors to the site.

*Ormaig: the east side of the lower decorated outcrop, with some of the 'rosettes' in the foreground*

# CAIRNBAAN

On a hillside overlooking Lochgilphead are two groups of richly carved rock outcrops, about 100m (330ft) apart.

Site 1 consists of three schistose outcrops carved with over 80 cups, mostly plain, but some having one or more rings. At one end of the outcrop several cups have grooves running downslope from them. One suggestion is that 'ancient priests' filled the cups with blood from sacrifices, letting it run over the rock via the connecting gutters.

Below *Cairnbaan Site 2 showing some conjoined cup-and-ring marks. On the left is a cup with 'rays' linking it to a single ring*

Above *Cairnbaan Site 1 with its cup markings, many linked by grooves*

# ACHNABRECK

At Achnabreck in Argyll is a series of cup-and-ring marked schist outcrops, the most impressive group of prehistoric carvings in Scotland.

Site 1 comprises three areas and is the largest of the sites. The lowest part of the outcrop has many multi-ringed cups, some with up to seven rings, many connected by grooves.

Thirty metres (100ft) uphill, the second site has the distinction of including some of the biggest cup-and-

**Right** *The cup-and-ring marks of Achnabreck 1's lower outcrop*

**Below** *One of the largest cup-and-ring marks, on the middle outcrop of Achnabreck 1*

*The upper outcrop of Achnabreck 1, showing the double spiral in the foreground*

ring marks in Scotland, almost 1m (3ft 3in) in diameter. A further 3m (10ft) on is an area with some very unusual and carefully executed designs. As well as a variety of cups and cup-and-ring marks, there is a double ended or horned spiral, and a set of three spirals.

Some of the motifs from Argyll and south-west Scotland, such as the spirals at Achnabreck, are similar to those on stones found at Irish passage graves, giving some clue as to their possible origin.

From careful study of Scotland's cup-and-ring marks, most researchers have concluded that the carvings on any one outcrop were the work of more than one artist, with symbols perhaps being added over a period of time.

At Achnabreck this would certainly seem to be the case. The highest part of the outcrop is carved with several of the 'Irish' motifs. These seem to have been partly covered by later carvings, adding weight to the theory that the initial idea for the designs may have come from Ireland. The occurrence of similar art in Brittany and the north coast of Spain indicates trade and contact between these areas via the western seaways.

# EPILOGUE

Scotland entered history with Tacitus' account of the Governor Gnaeus Julius Agricola's advance into the Lowlands of Scotland in AD 80. The Roman army constructed a succession of forts, joined by roads, reaching as far north as the Tay. This part of the campaign seems to have been relatively trouble-free, with the south of Scotland becoming part of the Roman Empire, apparently without a battle.

Agricola met more resistance in AD 84 when he advanced further north, however. Somewhere in

*The Craw Stane, Rhynie, Gordon, a Pictish symbol stone, incised with a fish and a 'beast'. In the background is the Tap o'Noth hillfort*

Left *The Clackmannan Stone, beside the tolbooth in Clackmannan, comprises a monolith with a whinstone boulder on top of it. The Manau were a local Iron Age tribe, and the boulder is thought to be connected with their ritual life, although it was only placed on top of the (probably Bronze Age) monolith last century*

Aberdeenshire, at a location known to Tacitus as 'Mons Graupius', his army clashed with the combined forces of the surrounding native tribes, about 30,000 men according to Tacitus. Despite their inferior numbers, the Romans won.

Consolidation of the victory was never brought about because Agricola's governorship ended, and soon afterwards many of the troops were called to the Danube to support the frontier. By about AD 100, all the forts of southern Scotland seem to have been abandoned. The Romans later consolidated their northern frontier in the 120s by building Hadrian's Wall between the Tyne and the Solway.

In AD 138, Q. Lollius Urbicus, the governor of Britain, received orders from the Emperor Antonius Pius to regain control of the south of Scotland, and Roman troops again advanced north. A new frontier was established through the building of the Antonine Wall, begun around AD 142. The Wall ran between the Firth of Forth and the Clyde, and had on its south side a road, the Military Way. This road ran between forts built at distances of about 3km (2 miles) apart for the length of the Wall. The Antonine Wall remained the northern frontier until the death of the Emperor in AD 161 when the frontier was abandoned for Hadrian's Wall.

Trouble flared up in Scotland again in the third century AD. The situation was serious enough to bring the Emperor Septimius Severus and his sons Caracalla and Geta with extra troops to sort out the offending tribes, the Maeatae and the Caledonii, who occupied parts of eastern and northern Scotland. An old base at Cramond was refortified, and a new base was built on the Tay, at Carpow. The Roman presence was felt as far north as the temporary camp at Keithock in Angus.

The tribes were subdued for a time, but soon revolted again. In AD 211 Septimus Severus died, and Caracalla returned to Rome. For about 100 years the Roman troops maintained a shaky peace from four forts, patrolling the area between Hadrian's Wall and the Tay.

Scotland was never truly 'Romanised' during this long period of invasion and retreat. The Roman presence would have been very much as an occupying force in the South, and in the North, it is probable that in many areas their presence was little felt. The main contact between the natives and Romans (apart from fighting) would have been trade, the large garrisons requiring fresh produce to supplement their imported supplies.

To the north of the Votadini, Selgovae, Novantae and Damnonii, the tribes occupying the south of Scotland, were the groups labelled the Picts and Scots.

The Picts are first mentioned in the historical sources in AD 297, by Eumenius, in his panegyric. 'Picti' may represent a Latinised version of the Picts' name for themselves, or the Roman's name for a 'painted people'. There are references to the inhabitants of northern Britain tattooing themselves and applying woad to their skins. Thus the Picts were not a new people, but the naming of existing groups, mainly the Caledonii and the Maeatae. Their territories were those north of the Forth–Clyde 'line', with their 'heartland' in east Scotland. The Picts are known mainly from their symbol stones and metalwork, and their cellular houses in the North.

A single Pictish kingdom developed sometime around AD 550. By this time the area corresponding to present-day Argyll was occupied by incomers from Ireland, the Scots. Most evidence for the Scots comes from their forts, such as Dunadd in Argyll, one of the strongholds of their kingdom of Dalriada.

In the south of Scotland at this time the most important centres on the east were probably Edinburgh, Stirling and Traprain Law, and on the west, Castle Rock, Dumbarton and the Mote of Mark, Kirkcudbright.

The following centuries saw the conversions of many of the inhabitants of Scotland to Christianity, the continued feuding of various tribes, and, by AD 800, the beginnings of Viking raiding and settlement in the north and south. In AD 843 the kingships of the Picts and Scots came under the leadership of one man, Kenneth MacAlpin, who formed the kingdom of Alba, taking in much of present-day Scotland.

# GLOSSARY

**Aisled round house** Late **Iron Age** stone built house, found mainly in the Northern Isles and Outer Hebrides. Similar to a **wheelhouse**, but the partitions are free-standing rather than adjoining the walls

**Amber** Fossilised tree resin, often used in antiquity for the manufacture of jewellery

**Anaerobic** Environment without free oxygen, that is, without the oxidation processes that lead to the decay of organic materials. Anaerobic environments, which can include waterlogged deposits such as peat bogs, provide favourable conditions for the preservation of organic materials such as wood and leather

**Ard** A 'scratch plough', which digs up the soil without turning it

**Artefact** An object made by man, such as a tool or weapon

**Awl** Bone, stone or metal point used to make holes

**Axe factory** Area of quarrying where the quarried rock was either partially or totally shaped into an axe before being transported

**Bar-hole** Space left between wall stones – at an entrance – into which a bar could be slotted, securing the door

**Batter** Inward slope given to an architectural feature, such as a double wall or ditch, to increase its stability

**Beaker** Type of pottery 'drinking vessel' often totally decorated with bands of incised and impressed patterns. Found in many parts of Europe, including Britain, in the early **Bronze Age**

**Blockhouse** Massively built stone structure, forming the 'gateway' to a fort, exhibiting characteristic **broch** features such as **guard cells** and **door checks**

**Brochs** Round tower-like drystone structures, confined mainly to the North and West of Scotland, and dating to the **Iron Age**

**Bronze Age** Period after the **Neolithic** and before the **Iron Age**. In Scotland dates from around 2000 BC to 500 BC. Characterised by the use of bronze for the manufacture of tools and weapons

**Burnt Mound** Pile of burnt stones, believed to have been used in the heating of food, often surrounding a cooking area

**Buttress** A projecting piece of walling, built to support an existing wall

**Capstone** Large stone which covers a burial cist or completes the roofing of a chamber

**Carbon 14** C14 or radiocarbon dating. A dating method to determine the age of organic substances, usually wood or bone in the case of archaeology. Levels of the radioactive isotope carbon 14 vary in proportion to the age of the sample

**Chambered Tomb** Tomb in which the burial chamber or chambers are located in the heart of a stone or earthen mound

**Chevaux de Frise** Short pillars of wood or stone set up around the entrance to a fort to impede an attack by horseback

**Cist** Stone-sided burial structure or box, the sides formed of slabs, dug into the ground and sometimes covered by a cairn of stones

**Clava Cairn** Localised type of cairn, found mainly in the area around Inverness, in which the burial cairn is often surrounded by a **stone circle**

**Clearance Cairn** Small heaps of stones found around the boundaries of former fields. Made during the preparation of ground for sowing

**Clyde Cairn** A type of chambered tomb – found in south-west Scotland – usually rectangular or trapezoidal in shape and having a forecourt leading to an elongated burial chamber partitioned by protruding slabs

**Corbelling** A roofing technique used in stone building in which each course of stonework in the walling protrudes slightly more than the one below, until all the walls either meet or come so close together that they can be spanned by a **capstone**

**Corracle** A small oval boat made from skins stretched on wickerwork

**Crannog** Lake dwelling, built on a small island which is often at least partly man-made

**Cup and Rings** Carvings, found either on rock faces or on the faces of standing stones or stones built into a tomb or other structure, comprising cups or hollows, sometimes surrounded by one or more carved rings. Most are thought to belong to the **Bronze Age**

**Dirk** A dagger

**Door Checks** Walls protruding at each side of an entrance passage, which stop a door from being pulled open from the outside. The door was drawn across the passage from the inside, being secured with a bar

**Drystone** Walling built without any cementing material. The stones are arranged carefully in courses, with smaller stones filling the gaps between

**Dun** Gaelic for 'a fortified place', but to archaeologists meaning a small **drystone** fort, usually dating to the **Iron Age** or later, and found mainly in the west of Scotland

**Facade** Setting of upright stones flanking the entrance to a chambered tomb

**Fibula** Brooch with a pin and clasp. Implies the wearing of a draped garment such as a cloak

**Flankers** The two stones which adjoin the prostrate stone in a **recumbent stone circle**. The flankers are often the tallest stones in the circle

**Flint** A hard 'glassy' rock which flakes easily and can be worked to produce a sharp cutting edge. Used in prehistoric times for the manufacture of tools and weapons such as scrapers and arrowheads

**Flint Scatter** Concentration of flints which have been worked by man, including debris from tool manufacture. Where settlement is suspected in an area without upstanding remains to help in its location, the area can be 'walked', and the density of flints used to pinpoint the most likely area of settlement

**Geo** A deep gully

**Geophysical Survey** Use of electronic equipment to locate sites by recording variations in the magnetism and resistivity of the soil

**Grooved Ware** Type of **Neolithic** pottery found in some parts of Scotland and England. It is decorated with patterns formed mainly of parallel lines or 'grooves' made either by incising the pattern onto the damp vessel, or by applying rolled up strips of clay to the unfired vessel

**Guard Cell** Small cell, often found at one or both sides of the entrance to a broch or dun, and assumed to have housed a person, or dog, guarding the door

**Hammerstone** Stone, often a river or beach pebble, which has been used as a pounding tool. Identified by patches of damage on one or both ends

**Hand-axe** Large multi-purpose tool, usually shaped from a core of flint or fine-grained rock

**Henge** Area, usually circular or eliptical, enclosed by a ditch and bank, the ditch being on the interior. Usually interpreted as a meeting place for ceremony and ritual. Often encloses a **stone circle**

**Hillfort** Hilltop enclosure fortified by one or more ramparts and ditches. Many contain the outlines of huts and were probably defended villages

**Hoard** Collection of materials, usually metal, deposited in the ground. Depending on the make-up and place of deposition of a hoard, it can usually be identified as a personal hoard (possessions buried in times of danger), a founder's hoard (miscast and worn objects and raw materials), a merchant's hoard (new objects) or a votive hoard (objects deposited in a 'sacred' place such as a lake)

**Horned Cairn** A burial cairn with projecting cairn material delineating a court in front of the entrance, and sometimes also at the 'back' of the cairn

**Hut Circle** Outline of the foundation, often stone, of a former hut, probably originally roofed with timber rafters and then thatched

**Iron Age** Final period of prehistory in Scotland, beginning around 500 BC, and lasting into the early centuries of the first millennium AD. Iron superceded bronze as the popular material for the manufacture of tools and weapons

**Isostatic Uplift** The post-glacial rising or rebound of land relative to the sea after the melting of heavy, overlying ice sheets

**Jamb** The post or sidepiece of a door

**Lintel** The large stone or wooden beam which spans the top of doorway or similar opening

**Mesolithic** 'Middle Stone Age'. The period between the **Palaeolithic** and **Neolithic**, from around 7000 BC to 4000 BC. The Mesolithic groups were hunter-gatherers like their predecessors, but their greater reliance on fishing and fowling seems to have given them a more sedentary lifestyle than the Palaeolithic groups who relied more on hunting large game. The **microlith** characterises their toolkit

**Microliths** Tiny tools made from a flake of flint or fine-grained rock. Often several were hafted on the same shaft to form a composite tool

**Midden** Deposit of household rubbish comprising fuel ash, animal bones, shells, broken pottery, discarded tools, and the like. Middens are usually found in the vicinity of settlement sites

**Monolith** Large freestanding stone

**Mortuary House** Wooden or stone structure used as a tomb, and buried under a barrow

**Neolithic** 'New Stone Age'. Period between the **Mesolithic** and the **Bronze Age**, in Scotland dating from around 4000 BC to 2000 BC. Characterised by the introduction of farming

**Orthostat** Large stone or slab, set vertically in a structure

**Palaeolithic** 'Old Stone Age'. In Britain it begins with the earliest occupation by man around 450,000 years ago, and ends with the **Mesolithic** around 7000 BC

**Palaeopathology** The study of disease, ailments, fracture, dental decay, etc. by the examination of marks on bones

**Palstave** Type of axe with side flanges and a 'stop ridge'

**Pollen Analysis** Study of pollen grains, preserved in the soil in certain conditions, such as in a peat bog. Used to identify plant species that can indicate environmental conditions when the deposit was laid down

**Portal Stones** Large stones forming the entrance to a structure, usually a tomb

**Posthole** Socket which would have held an upright post, either stone or timber. Even when a post has been removed or has decayed, its existence can usually be recognised during excavation by colour and texture changes in the soil

**Promontory Fort** Fort constructed by cutting off the end of a coastal promontory or inland eminence, with a thick **rampart** or wall defending the only easy line of approach

**Quarry Scoops** Depressions left in the ground after stone has been removed for building

**Quern** Coarse stones for grinding grain. The older form is the saddle quern, which has a larger bottom stone with a smaller top one for rubbing over the grain. The more recent form, the rotary quern, consisted of two round flat stones. The grain was placed between them and then the top stone was rotated by hand

**Rampart** Large bank of earth or stones or both forming the defences of a fortified site such as a **hillfort**

**Rapier** Similar weapon to a sword, but having a more slender blade. Would have been used for thrusting rather than slashing

**Recumbent Stone Circle** A **stone circle** in which one of the stones is prostrate. These circles are confined mainly to the area around Aberdeen

**Red Ochre** Red oxide of iron, occurring naturally and thought to have been used for painting the skin

**Scarcement** Ledge protruding from the wall of a building, its purpose being to hold the beams of an upper floor or roof

**Semi-Broch** Term used to describe some stone-built fortified structures in the west of Scotland, which it is thought show many of the features of a fully developed **broch**, and may be an advanced stage in their development

**Socketed Axe** Metal axe with a hole cast in it to take a haft

**Souterrain** Also called 'earth-house'. A long, underground passage, often having drystone walling and a flagged roof, and sometimes a chamber. Most were probably attached to a settlement, and used for storage

**Stalled Cairn** Chambered burial cairn, its long chamber partitioned by slabs

**Steatite** Soapstone. A soft rock sometimes carved into vessels

**Stone Circle** Circles or elipses of standing stones, most belonging to the Bronze Age, and believed to be connected with ritual

**Unstan Pottery** Shallow collared bowls, sometimes decorated below the rims, found in settlement and burial sites in the north of Scotland in the early **Neolithic** period

**Vitrified Fort** Fort in which the ramparts have been burnt at such high temperatures that the stones have been fused into a glassy mass

**Wag** Rectangular or round house, probably late **Iron Age** in date, in which the roofs were supported by rows of pillars

**Wheelhouse** Round drystone house, usually dated to the later **Iron Age**, in which partition walling, possibly roof supports, radiate in from the wall like the spokes of a wheel

# GAZETTEER

## Shetland

Burgi Geos blockhouse and fort,
Yell
HP 478034
o/s 1″ Map 1, 1:50,000 Map 1

Clickhimin settlement and broch,
Lerwick, Mainland
HBM (SDD)
HU 464408
o/s 1″ Map 4, 1:50,000 Map 4

Gruting School Neolithic house,
Walls, Mainland
HU 281498
o/s 1″ Map 2, 1:50,000 Map 3

Jarlshof settlement and broch,
Sumburgh Head, Mainland
HBM (SDD)
HU 398095
o/s 1″ Map 4, 1:50,000 Map 4

Mousa broch, Mousa
HBM (SDD)
HU 457206
o/s 1″ Map 4, 1:50,000 Map 4

Ness of Burgi fort and
blockhouse, Scatness, Mainland
HBM (SDD)
HU 388083
o/s 1″ Map 4, 1:50,000 Map 4

Pettigarth's Field Neolithic
settlement, Whalsay
HU 587652
o/s 1″ Map 3, 1:50,000 Map 2

Punds Water chambered tomb,
Brae, Mainland
HU 324712
o/s 1″ Map 2, 1:50,000 Map 3

Scord of Brouster Neolithic
settlement, Walls, Mainland
HU 255516
o/s 1″ Map 2, 1:50,000 Map 3

Stanydale Neolithic houses and
'temple', Walls, Mainland
HBM (SDD)
HU 285502
o/s 1″ Map 2, 1:50,000 Map 3

## Orkney

Brodgar, stone circle and henge,
Mainland
HBM (SDD)
HY 294133
o/s 1″ Map 6, 1:50,000 Map 6

Cuween chambered tomb,
Finstown, Mainland
HBM (SDD)
HY 364127
o/s 1″ Map 6, 1:50,000 Map 6

Dwarfie Stane, rock-cut tomb,
Hoy
HBM (SDD)
HY 243004
o/s 1″ Map 7, 1:50,000 Map 6

Grain souterrain, Kirkwall,
Mainland
HBM (SDD)
HY 441116
o/s 1″ Map 6, 1:50,000 Map 6

Gurness Broch, Sands of Evie,
Mainland
HBM (SDD)
HY 381268
o/s 1″ Map 6, 1:50,000 Map 6

Holm of Papa Westray (South)
chambered cairn, Papa Westray
HBM (SDD)
HY 509518
o/s 1″ Map 5, 1:50,000 Map 5

Isbister chambered tomb,
South Ronaldsay
ND 470845
o/s 1″ Map 7, 1:50,000 Map 7

Knap of Howar settlement,
Papa Westray
HBM (SDD)
HY 483518
o/s 1″ Map 5, 1:50,000 Map 5

Liddle burnt mound,
South Ronaldsay
ND 464841
o/s 1″ Map 7, 1:50,000 Map 7

Maes Howe chambered tomb,
Mainland
HBM (SDD)
HY 318127
o/s 1″ Map 6, 1:50,000 Map 6

Midhowe broch, Rousay
HBM (SDD)
HY 371306
o/s 1″ Map 6, 1:50,000 Map 6

Midhowe stalled cairn, Rousay
HBM (SDD)
HY 372304
o/s 1″ Map 6, 1:50,000 Map 6

Quoyness chambered tomb,
Sanday
HBM (SDD)
HY 676377
o/s 1″ Map 5, 1:50,000 Map 5

Rennibister souterrain, Kirkwall,
Mainland
HBM (SDD)
HY 397125
o/s 1″ Map 6, 1:50,000 Map 6

Skara Brae Neolithic settlement,
Bay of Skaill, Mainland
HBM (SDD)
HY 231187
o/s 1″ Map 6, 1:50,000 Map 6

Stenness, stone circle and henge,
Mainland
HBM (SDD)
HY 306125
o/s 1″ Map 6, 1:50,000 Map 6

Taversoe Tuick chambered tomb,
Rousay
HBM (SDD)
HY 425276
o/s 1″ Map 6, 1:50,000 Map 6

Unstan chambered tomb,
Mainland
HBM (SDD)
HY 282117
o/s 1″ Map 6, 1:50,000 Map 6

Wideford Hill chambered tomb,
Mainland
HBM (SDD)
HY 409121
o/s 1″ Map 6, 1:50,000 Map 6

## Western Isles

### Lewis
Dun Carloway, broch, Carloway
HBM (SDD)
NB 190413
o/s 1″ Map 12, 1:50,000 Map 8

Callanish stone circles and
standing stones, Callanish
HBM (SDD)
Callanish I NB 213331
Callanish II NB 222326
Callanish III NB 225326
Callanish IV NB 230304
o/s 1″ Map 12, 1:50,000 Map 13

### North Uist
Barpa Langass chambered cairn,
Clachan
NF 837657
o/s 1″ Map 17, 1:50,000 Map 18

Clettraval wheelhouse settlement,
Tigharry
NF 749713
o/s 1″ Map 17, 1:50,000 Map 18

Dun Torcuill broch, Loch an Duin
NF 888737
o/s 1″ Map 17, 1:50,000 Map 18

Unival chambered tomb,
Kirkibost
NF 800668
o/s 1″ Map 17, 1:50,000 Map 18

## Highland

### Caithness
Achavanich stone setting,
Loch Stemster
ND 187417
o/s 1″ Map 11, 1:50,000 Map 12

Camster chambered cairns,
Watten
HBM (SDD)
Long cairn ND 260442
Round cairn ND 260440
o/s 1″ Map 16, 1:50,000 Map 12

Cnoc Freiceadain, chambered long
cairns, Reay
HBM (SDD)
ND 012653
o/s 1″ Map 11, 1:50,000 Map 12

Forse wag, broch and settlement,
Latheron
ND 204352
o/s 1″ Map 11 (also 15 and 16),
1:50,000 Map 11

Garrywhin horned cairn (Cairn of
Get), Ulbster
HBM (SDD)
ND 313411
o/s 1″ Map 16, 1:50,000 Map 12

Mid Clyth stone rows
(Hill o'Many Stanes)
HBM (SDD)
ND 295384
o/s 1″ Map 16, 1:50,000 Map 11

### Sutherland
Carn Liath broch, Golspie
HBM (SDD)
NC 870013
o/s 1″ Map 22, 1:50,000 Map 17

Clachtoll broch, Lochinver
NC 036278
o/s 1″ Map 13, 1:50,000 Map 15

Coille na Borgie chambered long
cairns, Strathnaver
NC 715590
o/s 1″ Map 10, 1:50,000 Map 10

Dun Dornadilla broch,
Atnacaillich, Loch Hope
HBM (SDD)
NC 457450
o/s 1″ Map 9, 1:50,000 Map 9

Dun na Maigh broch,
Kyle of Tongue
NC 552530
o/s 1″ Map 10, 1:50,000 Map 10

Kilphedir broch, Helmsdale
NC 994189
o/s 1″ Map 15, 1:50,000 Map 17

Kilphedir hut circles, Helmsdale
NC 991190
o/s 1″ Map 15, 1:50,000 Map 17

Laid souterrain, Durness
NC 428612
o/s 1″ Map 9, 1:50,000 Map 9

**Inverness**

Clava cairns, Balnuaran of Clava
HBM (SDD)
NH 757444 area
o/s 1″ Map 28, 1:50,000 Map 27

Corrimony chambered cairn,
Glen Urquhart
HBM (SDD)
NH 383303
o/s 1″ Map 27, 1:50,000 Map 26

**Skye and Lochalsh**

*Skye*
Dun Ardtreck, dun, Carbost
NG 335358
o/s 1″ Map 24, 1:50,000 Map 32

Dun Beag, broch, Struan
HBM (SDD)
NG 339386
o/s 1″ Map 24, 1:50,000 Map 32

Dun Gerashader, promontory
dun, Portree
NG 489453
o/s 1″ Map 25, 1:50,000 Map 23

Dun Grugaig, dun, Elgol
NG 535124
o/s 1″ Map 34, 1:50,000 Map 32

Rudh, an Dunain chambered
tomb, Glen Brittle
NG 393163
o/s 1″ Map 33, 1:50,000 Map 32

Vatten chambered tombs,
Loch Caroy
NG 297440
o/s 1″ Map 24, 1:50,000 Map 23

*Lochalsh*
Caisteal Grugaig broch, Totaig
NG 867251
o/s 1″ Map 26, 1:50,000 Map 33

Dun Grugaig dun, Glenelg
NG 851159
o/s 1″ Map 35, 1:50,000 Map 33

Dun Telve broch, Glenelg
HBM (SDD)
NG 829172
o/s 1″ Map 35, 1:50,000 Map 33

Dun Troddan broch, Glenelg
HBM (SDD)
NG 833172
o/s 1″ Map 35, 1:50,000 Map 33

## Grampian

**Banff and Buchan**
Memsie round cairn, Fraserburgh
HBM (SDD)
NJ 976620
o/s 1″ Map 31, 1:50,000 Map 30

Strichen recumbent stone circle,
Fraserburgh
NJ 936544
o/s 1″ Map 31, 1:50,000 Map 30

**Gordon**
Broomend of Crichie henge,
Inverurie
NJ 779196
o/s 1″ Map 40, 1:50,000 Map 38

Craw Stane Pictish symbol stone,
Rhynie
NJ 497263
o/s 1″ Map 39, 1:50,000 Map 37

Cullerlie standing stones, Echt
HBM (SDD)
NJ 785042
o/s 1″ Map 40, 1:50,000 Map 38

Dunnideer hillfort and castle,
Insch
NJ 612281
o/s 1″ Map 39, 1:50,000 Map 37

Easter Aquhorthies, recumbent
stone circle, Inverurie
HBM (SDD)
NJ 732207
o/s 1″ Map 40, 1:50,000 Map 38

Loanhead of Daviot,
recumbent stone circle and
enclosed cremation cemetery,
Old Meldrum
HBM (SDD)
NJ 747288
o/s 1″ Map 40, 1:50,000 Map 38

Midmar Kirk recumbent stone
circle, Echt
NJ 699064
o/s 1″ Map 40, 1:50,000 Map 38

Sunhoney recumbent stone circle,
Echt
NJ 715056
o/s 1″ Map 40, 1:50,000 Map 38

Tap o'Noth hillfort, Rhynie
NJ 484293
o/s 1″ Map 39, 1:50,000 Map 37

**Kincardine and Deeside**
Capo long barrow, Inglismaldie
Forest
NO 633664
o/s 1″ Map 43, 1:50,000 Map 45

New Kinord settlement, Dinnet
NJ 449001
o/s 1″ Map 42, 1:50,000 Map 44

## Tayside

**Perth and Kinross**
Newbigging cup and ring stone
NO 155352
o/s 1″ Map 49, 1:50,000 Map 53

Orwell standing stones, Loch
Leven
NO 149043
o/s 1″ Map 55, 1:50,000 Map 58

**Angus**
Ardestie souterrain, Dundee
HBM (SDD)
NO 502344
o/s 1″ Map 50, 1:50,000 Map 54

Barns of Airlie souterrain, Alyth
NO 305515
o/s 1″ Map 49, 1:50,000 Map 53

Brown and White Caterthun
forts, Brechin
HBM (SDD)
Brown Caterthun NO 555668
White Caterthun NO 547660
o/s 1″ Map 50, 1:50,000 Map 44

Carlungie 1 souterrain, Dundee
HBM (SDD)
NO 511359
o/s 1″ Map 50, 1:50,000 Map 54

Finavon vitrified fort, Forfar
NO 506556
o/s 1″ Map 50, 1:50,000 Map 54

## *Fife*

### Kirkcaldy
Balbirnie stone circle, Glenrothes
NO 285029
o/s 1″ Map 56, 1:50,000 Map 59

Balfarg henge, Glenrothes
NO 281031
o/s 1″ Map 56, 1:50,000 Map 59

### North East Fife
Lundin Links standing stones,
Largo Bay
NO 404027
o/s 1″ Map 56, 1:50,000 Map 59

## *Strathclyde*

### Clydesdale
Arbory Hill fort, Abington
NS 944238
o/s 1″ Map 68, 1:50,000 Map 72

Corbury Hill unenclosed platform
settlement, Crawford
NS 967210
o/s 1″ Map 68, 1:50,000 Map 72

Normangill Rig unenclosed
platform settlement, Crawford
NS 966215
o/s 1″ Map 68, 1:50,000 Map 72

Ritchie Ferry settlement,
Crawford
NS 945215
o/s 1″ Map 68, 1:50,000 Map 72

### Argyll
Achnabreck cup and rings,
Lochgilphead
HBM (SDD)
NR 856907
o/s 1″ Map 52, 1:50,000 Map 55

Ardanaiseig crannog, Loch Awe
NN 091249
o/s 1″ Map 53, 1:50,000 Map 50

Ardifur dun, Kilmartin
NR 789969
o/s 1″ Map 52, 1:50,000 Map 55

Ballochroy standing stones and
cist, Kintyre
NR 730525
o/s 1″ Map 58, 1:50,000 Map 62

Ballymeanoch standing stones,
Kilmartin Valley
NR 833965
o/s 1″ Map 52, 1:50,000 Map 55

Baluachraig cup and rings,
Kilmartin Valley
HBM (SDD)
NR 832969
o/s 1″ Map 52, 1:50,000 Map 55

Beacharra standing stone, Killean,
Kintyre
NR 692433
o/s 1″ Map 65, 1:50,000 Map 62

Cairnbaan cup and rings,
Kilmartin Valley
HBM (SDD)
NR 838910
o/s 1″ Map 52, 1:50,000 Map 55

Corriechrevie cairn, Clachan,
Kintyre
NR 738540
o/s 1″ Map 58, 1:50,000 Map 62

Kintraw, standing stones and
cairns
NM 830050
o/s 1″ Map 52, 1:50,000 Map 55

Nether Largie burial cairns,
Kilmartin Valley
Nether Largie South: NR 828979
Nether Largie Mid: NR 830983
Nether Largie North: NR 830984
HBM (SDD)
o/s 1″ Map 52, 1:50,000 Map 55

Nether Largie standing stones,
Kilmartin Valley
NR 827977
o/s 1″ Map 52, 1:50,000 Map 55

Ormaig cup and rings, Mid Argyll
NM 822026
o/s 1″ Map 52, 1:50,000 Map 55

Ri Cruin cairn, Kilmartin Valley
HBM (SDD)
NR 825971
o/s 1″ Map 52, 1:50,000 Map 55

Strontoiller standing stone and
cairn, Lorn
NM 907289
o/s 1″ Map 52, 1:50,000 Map 49

Temple Wood stone circle,
Kilmartin Valley
HBM (SDD)
NR 826978
o/s 1″ Map 52, 1:50,000 Map 55

### Cunninghame

*Arran*
Auchagallon cairn/stone circle,
Machrie Moor
HBM (SDD)
NR 893346
o/s 1″ Map 66, 1:50,000 Map 69

Machrie Moor stone circles
HBM (SDD)
NR 910324 area
o/s 1″ Map 66, 1:50,000 Map 69

## Central

### Clackmannan
Clackmannan Stone,
Clackmannan
NS 911918
o/s 1″ Map 55, 1:50,000 Map 58

## Dumfries and Galloway

### Wigtown
Cairnholy chambered tombs,
Creetown
HBM (SDD)
Cairnholy I: NX 517538
Cairnholy II: NX 518540
o/s 1″ Map 73 and 80, 1:50,000
Map 83

Kemp's Walk, promontory fort,
Broadsea Bay
NW 975598
o/s 1″ Map 79, 1:50,000 Map 82

Torhousekie stone circle,
Bladnoch Valley
HBM (SDD)
NX 382564
o/s 1″ Map 80, 1:50,000 Map 83

### Stewarty
Castle Haven dun, Borgue
NX 593482
o/s 1″ Map 80, 1:50,000 Map 83

High Banks cup and rings,
Kirkcudbright
NX 709489
o/s 1″ Map 81, 1:50,000 Map 84

### Nithsdale
Twelve Apostles stone circle,
Newbridge
NX 947794
o/s 1″ Map 74, 1:50,000 Map 84

Tynron Doon fort, Penpont
NX 819939
o/s 1″ Map 74, 1:50,000 Map 78

### Annandale and Eskdale
Burnswark Hill fort, Ecclefechan
NY 185785
o/s 1″ Map 75, 1:50,000 Map 85

## Lothian

### East Lothian
The Chesters fort, Drem
HBM (SDD)
NT 507782
o/s 1″ Map 63, 1:50,000 Map 66

Green Castle fort, Gifford
NT 582657
o/s 1″ Map 63, 1:50,000 Map 66

North Berwick Law hillfort
NT 555842
o/s 1″ Map 63, 1:50,000 Map 66

### West Lothian
Cairnpapple Hill
HBM (SDD)
NS 987717
o/s 1″ Map 61, 1:50,000 Map 65

## Borders

### Berwick
Edinshall broch, Duns
HBM (SDD)
NT 772603
o/s 1″ Map 64, 1:50,000 Map 67

Mutiny Stones long cairn,
Longformacus
NT 622590
o/s 1″ Map 63, 1:50,000 Map 67

### Tweeddale
Cademuir forts, Peebles
Cademuir I: NT 230374
Cademuir II: NT 224370
o/s 1″ Map 69, 1:50,000 Map 73

Dreva Craig hillfort, Broughton
NT 126353
o/s 1″ Map 69, 1:50,000 Map 72

### Ettrick and Lauderdale
Eildon Hill North fort, Melrose
NT 555328
o/s 1″ Map 70, 1:50,000 Map 73

### Roxburgh
Woden Law fort, Jedburgh
NT 768125
o/s 1″ Map 70, 1:50,000 Map 80

# FURTHER READING

Barber, J. and Magee, D.A., 1987, *Innsegall*. John Donald

Bray, W. and Tramp, D., 1972, *The Penguin Dictionary of Archaeology*. Penguin

Burl, A., 1981, *Rites of the Gods*. J.M. Dent

Burl, A., 1976, *The Stone Circles of the British Isles*. Yale University Press

Clarke, D.V., Cowie, T.G. and Foxon, A., 1985, *Symbols of Power at the Time of Stonehenge*. HMSO

Darvill, T., 1987, *Prehistoric Britain*. Batsford

Feachem, R.W., 1977 (2nd edn.), *Guide to Prehistoric Scotland*. Batsford

Henshall, A.S., 1963, 1972 (2 vols.), *The Chambered Tombs of Scotland*. Edinburgh University Press

MacKie, E.W., 1975, *Scotland: An Archaeological Guide*. Faber and Faber

MacSween, A., 1985, *The Brochs, Duns and Enclosures of Skye. Northern Archaeology*, vols 5 and 6

Morrison, I., 1985, *Landscape with Lake Dwellings*. Edinburgh University Press

Morris, R.W.B., 1979, *The Prehistoric Rock Art of Galloway and the Isle of Man*. Blandford Press

Renfrew, A.C., 1979, *Investigations in Orkney*. Society of Antiquaries of London

Renfrew, C., (ed), 1985, *The Prehistory of Orkney*. Edinburgh University Press

Ritchie, A., 1988, *Scotland BC*. HMSO

Ritchie, J.N.G. and Ritchie, A., 1981, *Scotland: Archaeology and Early History*. Thames and Hudson

Ritchie, J.N.G. and Ritchie, A., 1978, *The Ancient Monuments of Orkney*. HMSO

Royal Commission on the Ancient and Historical Monuments of Scotland, *Inventories* for Argyll, vols 1–6, (1971, 1975, 1980, 1982, 1984, 1988), Berwickshire (1915), Caithness (1911), Clackmannan (1933), Dumfriesshire (1920), East Lothian (1924), Edinburgh (1951), Fife (1933), Kirkcudbright (1914), Lanarkshire (1978), Midlothian (1929), Orkney (1946), Peebleshire (1967), Roxburgh (1956), Selkirkshire (1957), Shetland (1946), Stirlingshire (1963), Sutherland (1911), Western Isles and Skye (1928), West Lothian (1929), Wigtownshire (1912).

Royal Commission on the Ancient and Historical Monuments of Scotland, *Exploring Scotland's Heritage*, 8 vols. – Argyll and the Western Isles (1985), The Clyde Estuary and Central Region (1985), Lothian and the Borders (1985), Orkney and Shetland (1985), Dumfries and Galloway (1986), Grampian (1986), The Highlands (1986), Fife and Tayside (1987). HMSO

Smith, B., (ed), 1985, *Shetland Archaeology*. The Shetland Times

Thom, A., 1971, *Megalithic Lunar Observatories*. Oxford University Press

Wainwright, F.T., 1963, *The Souterrains of Southern Pictland*. Routledge and Kegan Paul

Such journals as the *Proceedings of the Society of Antiquaries of Scotland* and the *Glasgow Archaeological Journal* are also rich sources of information

# INDEX

Bold type indicates individual site entries.
*Italic* indicates illustrations.